A BUCKET OF STEAM

Captain Joe Earl, MNM

ARTHUR H. STOCKWELL LTD
Torrs Park, Ilfracombe, Devon, EX34 8BA
Established 1898
www.ahstockwell.co.uk

ISBN 978-0-7223-5053-9
Printed in Great Britain by
Arthur H. Stockwell Ltd
Torrs Park   Ilfracombe
Devon EX34 8BA

IN MEMORY

In special memory of my brother John, 1930–2004

A fine seaman and bosun, he served on many ships during his time at sea. Among them were the MV *King Steven*, MV *Baron Inverclyde*, SS *Consuelo*, MV *Sacramento*, SS *Merchant Knight*, SS *Dorrington Court*, SS *Beechwood*, SS *Rinaldo*, SS *Athel Knight*, SS *Ariosto*, SS *Saint Thomas*, and the *Sir Arthur Kennedy*.

FOREWORD

(by the Reverend Philip Auden, MNM, MNI, DL; vice-president, National Merchant Navy Association; padre, Bristol & District, Pill and North Somerset branches, MNA)

It is a tremendous pleasure for me to write the foreword for Captain Joe Earl's new compilation of writings and poems.

After a working life spent at sea, Joe brings to his writing a personal understanding of those 'who go down to the sea in ships'. He is able to evoke a whole range of maritime emotions and give us, the readers, the opportunity to be 'alongside' those characters and situations about which he writes.

I have had the opportunity of using Joe's previous works in sermons and memorial services, and I have even recorded a selection for group use. Always they are well received and stir up that affection for the sea and love of all things nautical that is a part of our island culture.

A SAILOR'S LAMENT

Gulls have pecked my eyes out, fish have cleaned my bones –
A man's recycled this way, in the locker of D. Jones.
Me and many shipmates, all were heaven-sent,
To cross the bar in silence – in liquid monument,

Finished with our human form and all the earthly strife,
Now biding midst the briny in our salty afterlife.
Whether you just paddle, or sail across the sea,
Please treat the water kindly – it could be partly me!

A SEAFARER'S PRAYER

Oh, Lord above, please keep an eye
On all seafarers sailing by.
Some are soft or hard as nails,
But seek Thy love when all else fails.

If while steaming shore to shore
We lose the fight – to endure
Certain perils, day or night –
Then we pray to see the light.

We may be selfish, scared, exposed,
Humbled now by human woes,
Since passing by the harbour trees,
To facing death in endless seas.

If by fate our days are numbered,
Set heaven's course unencumbered.
Whether sinner, near or far,
Please guide us, Lord, across the bar.

A SEAMAN'S iPOD

We used a windy hammer and oft a marlinspike;
A thimble in the bosun's vice closed a splice up tight.
We often dipped a sounding rod and cleaned a mucky strum;
Perhaps, perchance at noon, a well-earned shot of rum.

On the bridge a sextant for shooting of the stars,
The sound of engine's rhythm through the fiddly bars.
It may sound complicated, but we knew just what we did,
From streaming of a log to banging in a fid.

Now I have an iPod, wondering what's in store –
My memory and eyesight complicate it more.
It's connected to a router by a Wi-Fi thing somehow,
So I press this little button – I'm up and running now.

It again sounds complicated till once you learn the ropes!
Successful in a geeky way raising of your hopes,
It's definitely handy for doing many things:
Just google in a question – see what magic brings.

I had to put a password in – as a rule of thumb,
Thought I'd name it 'PENIS' as a bit of fun.
iPad didn't like it though – complaining it's too short –
So had to find a longer one and my idea abort.

I don't know what 4G is, or other things just yet,
But I can get quite quickly the bookies for a bet.
So, you see, old shellbacks, it's maybe worth a go,
Adding to your knowledge of ships so long ago.

ABANDON SHIP

Many shoreside people when they hear "Abandon ship"
Think perhaps it's easy, an exciting fun day trip,
Just ambling down the gangway and stepping in a boat;
But, my friend, believe me – the chance of that's remote.

Especially in the wartime with sinkings every day,
With very fraught conditions in each and every way,
Any time, throughout sunshine, or night till dusky dawn,
With no choice of the weather, in calm to violent storm,

Your ship becomes a victim, so thoughts run through your head.
'Shall I find my shipmates? Are they maimed or dead?
Better grab my cigarettes – wrap 'em watertight.
Is the enemy still waiting to kill us all for spite?

'Should I try to put the fire out, that's blazing on the deck?
Am I wasting time, if the ship's a total wreck?
Shall I jump overboard, and swim beneath the oil,
Before I'm blown asunder and depart this mortal coil?

'I may not hear "Abandon ship" or any firm dismissal,
If there is a smashed-up bridge or no steam on the whistle.
Where the hell's my life jacket? That I mustn't spurn.
The vessel now is listing and sinking by the stern.'

It reminds me of the trenches when rivets fly nearby,
Or in amongst the Blitz when bombs drop from the sky.
If you escape from that, you may just walk away,
But it is a little different with an ocean to survey.

If you're not incinerated, blind and choked by fuel,
Attacked by barracuda or drowned in sea so cruel,
Suffer thirst or sunstroke, or madness from despair,
Run down or crushed by 'rescuers' – then all you have is prayer.

Hauled into a lifeboat – escaping from the flame –
"OK, lads, get pulling! Which way's the shipping lane?
A thousand miles from nowhere – did a mayday call go off?
Is that a lurking U-boat spied in a leeward trough?"

Three weeks it was we rowed across the lurching heaving seas,
In spite of constant bailing with salt water to our knees,
Subsisting on bare rations and tins of marmalade.
Six of us survived that trip – the memory does not fade.

However, I was lucky, restored to my life of bliss,
Thought I'd speak to Joe; he could write it down – like this!

Swinging the lamp one night, the above observations were noted.

ADVICE TO A YOUNG MAN

Grab this life while you may, son – go abroad, see what you can,
For this world quickly changes as you grow into a man.

So many things you'd best do – while fit and in your prime.
Take things at the flood, young lad, ahead of Father Time.

Don't wait until your older – and reap the mental pain
Of lamenting wasted youth, and wanting time again.

A SHIP'S COOK

A cook will share the hazards of most things maritime,
In a cramped and pitching galley that's rolling all the time.
He suffers too from burns and scalds, or splashes from the fat,
And no stranger to the food poisoning, tasting from a vat.

Going back to old days aboard the sailing ships,
Staple grub was dry hash before they thought of chips.
The cook would boil up salt beef to go with musty bread –
Perhaps there were some dry peas immersed with pork instead.

The coffee made from green beans failed to satisfy –
A boiled-up weak infusion, but hot, to get them by.
All was pretty awful, I think you may agree,
If living on the rations they doled out there at sea.

The test of every sea cook was the making of his duff.
He used some grease or suet, mixing up the stuff
With a dollop of molasses among the weevily flour,
Then forced it in a canvas bag, then boiled it by the hour.

Sometimes he added raisins – he would call them plums –
To make this heavy pudding that stuck hard to the gums.
It wouldn't stop the scurvy, but beat the tack they knew.
A special dish on Sunday – a treat for all the crew.

AFTER THE PARADE

On Poppy Day our merchant men turned to at the square,
Along with other forces that also gathered there,
To honour all the fallen ones that lay neath ground or sea,
'Specially the sailors and some well known to me.
We'd dusted down our blazers an' polished up our boots,
Then we steamed through Bristol – to the bugle's toots.
This then made us thirsty, so we steered towards the pub.
It wasn't very far away, an' it also held the grub.
After the parade.

The King Billy was the venue – the very place to meet
After tramping round the centre, to the drummer's beat.
The ladies hove to first, you know – they were at the fore,
So when the landlord opened up they were stemming by the door.
We ordered up a pint or two and spoke of when we marched,
Then we sunk another one – cos most of us were parched.
The Sunday lunch was served to us, after climbing up the stairs,
Preceded by the red and white – the bottles came in pairs.
After the parade.

We sported all our medals, especially worn today.
It's great to see them shine like that – for the MNA.
There are many more I have not seen – this I do regret.
What can you do with men like these? They haven't claimed 'em yet.
A toast was drunk to absent friends – not without emotion –
And all the wives and family, too, remembered with devotion.
This is why, with heads held high, we convoyed mighty proud.
Not one of us – with lump in throat – denied the loyal crowd.
After the parade.

Amusing yarns were heard by all, and the speeches met by cheers,
During this Remembrance Day while dining with our peers.
Veterans are a special breed – they don't need perdition –
So we'll go round the buoy again, and continue the tradition.
Life is delight in simple things and we owe it to our friends.
True laughter has no bitter springs, so we take it to the ends.
But when you view it sideways we're not just here to drink.
One reason that we marched today was to make the nation think!
After the parade.

APART

Do you ever think of girlfriends, mothers and the wives
That remain at home and worry while men are risking lives?
It is an added burden to other tasks at home –
A kind of grief I'd call it, struggling there alone.

Holding hard the tears as they step out the door,
Perhaps to sail the seas or fight a crazy war.
They tell you that it won't be long – will seem like very soon –
And anyway, while looking up you'll see the same old moon.

They don't get the medals – those that stay and wait.
They receive a sentence until a far-off date.
I salute the women who brave their lives apart,
With the ache of separation and nearly broken heart.

ALFIE AND ME

Alfie and me on the poop deck jawing about the war.
We didn't see it coming – we never heard a roar.
Tin fish blew our tanker up, then it wasn't there –
Found ourselves in the 'oggin after flying in the air.

The sea afire and burning – we were in the clear.
Just me and him went diving – nobody else was near.
Alfie found some flotsam – his arm hooked round a spar.
He could hear me swearing – I wasn't away too far.

He flippered his way towards me and grabbed me by my shirt,
Bent me to the timber – told him I was hurt.
"Not a night for swimming," he bellows with a grin.
"Not", says I, just gasping, "wiv arf me ribs stove in."

I feared of what would happen, striving to stay afloat.
Atlantic cold – near freezing – and oil had reached my throat.
Alfie was out of the stokehold – a stubborn beggar was he.
(I was one of the deck crowd; he had cottoned on to me.)

For hours and hours he held me, 'most drowned and body aching.
Without a doubt he saved me, through the dawn a-breaking.
I was finished with engines, ready to chuck it all in;
Alfie it was that chivvied, with jokes as bad as sin.

I figured we should pray, in case we might survive,
But he didn't think that prayers would keep us both alive.
He said he knew no hymns, cos he'd never shipped on liners.
What he reckoned was – a collection for the miners.

Alfie weren't religious – he didn't have to be.
Just a merchant seaman living his life at sea,
One o' them men that won't give in – fighting till the end.
Lucky for me an' proud to be his mucker and a friend!

By and by a ship came up with a navy navigator.
He'd steamed away to chase a sub, but marked our spot for later.
There's only me and Alfie came through that mighty blast.
I spoke a silent prayer – for the mate who held me fast.

From a true yarn told to me by Alfie's mate some fifteen years after the event.

APOLLO

I reckon that I loved my work with energy and pride,
Aboard the old *Apollo* until our trade just died.
Redundant in my prime, my life could not redeem –
That's the only reason I left the Bristol Steam.

It's well I do remember that black and awful day,
When the owners gave me orders to take my ship away.
They sold her to some foreigners, so ending up my dream,
And flew a different house flag of unfamiliar green.

I sailed with other companies that answered to my call,
Losing touch with loyal crew – I missed them one and all.
I was the man that led the band with mighty high esteem,
But remember now the good old days aboard the Bristol Steam.

ARTIST, FIND YOUR BRUSHES

Please, artist, find your brushes;
Get your palette out for me
And paint for us a picture
Of a clipper on the sea –

A rakish topsail schooner,
Canvas billowed tight,
Bowsprit pointing over,
Gulls in swooping flight,

Running free or tacking,
A pitching speedy craft,
Black hull wet and shining,
Bubbling wake abaft.

She'll be pushing for a record
Of passage time at sea,
Racing home from China,
And her cargo is rich tea.

Slicing through the waves,
Her bow extreme and sharp,
Flying our red ensign
It's the famous *Cutty Sark*.

Please paint for me this picture,
This true historic scene,
Where sky is blue with sunshine
And the sea a topaz green.

AUSTRALIA

I flew back from Australia where mosquitoes suck one's blood,
And the pesky fruit flies crawl between the grub,
While staying on the east coast, in part of New South Wales,
A little in from Lennox Head, 'tween scrub and rolling dales.

Where the rollers from the ocean come crashing on the beach,
And the mandarins and mangoes picked with easy reach,
I gloried in the swimming and floating on the surf,
Hoped to back some winners on Sydney's distant turf.

Deadly brown snakes squirming upon the open ground;
The searing sun with burning wind, and lizards all around.
Between the trees the spiders swing to make a fatal web,
Then chase across to flies that stick and render them quite dead.

The earthy croak of dark-green frogs lurking in the drain;
The cut-short grass of gardens sorely needing rain;
Fruit so sweet and plentiful, eaten with the bran;
The fish and tasty salad, to sate the inner man.

In a local paddock, the cattle on the hoof;
The well-fed beaky egrets perching on the roof;
The purple tinge of sunset, at the start of night,
Merging with old Byron Bay against its loom of light.

The boxing stance of kangaroos looking for a fight;
Sturdy trunks of gum trees bleached a faded white;
Watered lawns all perfect mid unfamiliar flowers,
And lazing on a sunbed for many peaceful hours.

Yarning on verandas with a joking friendly mucker,
Quaffing ice-cold schooners, with a bite of tucker;
In the hazy distance the range of Burringbar;
The whistling of the butcher-birds returning calls so far.

The Southern Cross just hanging there early in the morn,
Afore the screech of parakeets at the break of dawn,
Plus the Aussie hospitality where I went to stay –
These things I remember since I flew away.

Now I'm back in England I recall that land of wonder
When I don my slouch hat – the one with corks down under.
I'm thinking they were used to me – no more a whinging Pom,
Just nodded heads and muttered *"There goes a To and From."*

March 2002

AUSTRALIAN MERCHANT NAVY

They were reluctant heroes – our seamen in the wars.
They came from all Australia and rallied round the cause.
A dangerous job in peacetime, they continued just the same;
During war afloat, my friends – through the shock and flame.

Australians at sea – officers and ranks –
Deserve a special mention and our heartfelt thanks,
For they served their country, sailing there and back,
Hauling vital cargoes in times that looked so black.

These doughty merchant seamen knew their cruel fate,
When struck by cunning sea wolves or mines left in their wake,
The *Limerick* and *Portmar*, *Recina*, *William Dawes*,
Dureenbee, *Wollonbar* – all sunk around our shores.

The *Kalingo*, the *Nimbin* and the *Iron Crown*,
The *Millimul* and others, amid the ships sent down,
Many fine Australians lost their lives back then,
Unsung and defenceless – we will remember them.

Countless were our heroes in the war at sea;
Inherent were the perils, and it seems to me
They carried out their duties – held the country fast.
Mariners of 'Aussie' – dauntless to the last!

BAMSE, 1937–1944
(Pronounced 'Bum-sa')

There's many a dog that went to sea, but one of fine renown
Was a hound that sailed with Norske Marine based at Montrose town,
He was a huge St Bernard, who fought in World War Two,
Owned by Captain Hafto, who signed him on as crew.

Bamse was a great dog, braver more than most,
Serving on a minesweeper, fearless at his post.
Wearing his tin helmet, he growled at German planes,
Standing by the Oerlikon among the shot and flames.

Word spread of his devotion and indifference under fire,
His exploits and adventures in those days so dire.
He saved a man from drowning, barking an alarm,
Jumping in the water then grabbing hold an arm.

He often caught a bus while roaming round alone,
Looking like he owned the place, steaming on his own.
Calling in a public house, he'd shove the cat aside,
Slurping then a brew that someone else supplied.

He visited the local shops, idling for a snack.
Children would adore him and ride upon his back.
He sometimes played in goal, when fooling on the grass,
But, guardian of the gangway, he'd let no stranger pass.

He padded round the pubs before the night curfew,
Escorting back to duty his often rowdy crew.
One night he met a robber threatening human life,
So pushed him in the dock for brandishing a knife.

More than just a mascot and fighting seaman too,
He was a morale booster, tangible and true.
A statue of brave Bamse stands at the waterside –
One tribute to a man's best friend, remembered here with pride.

BARRY DOCK: LOADING COAL

Barry Dock was opened in 1889.
Crucial was the need at that specific time.
Exporting coal 'most everywhere, Barry had no peer,
Exceeding even Cardiff, along the coast near here.

From pits within the valleys, the black stuff rumbled down,
By railway through to Cadoxton and on to Barry town.
The owners sent the captains with their empty ships
To load these bulky cargoes, underneath the tips.

The collier pumped out ballast and gangway put ashore,
Then took on her freight with a dusty crashing roar.
One by one the coal trucks were emptied down the chute,
While hard men trimmed the vessel and cargo holds to suit.

Finished off and loaded, the mate would note her draught,
The crew turned to, washing down, hosing fore and aft,
Shifted to a lay-by berth or mooring side by side,
Battened down and ready to sail the ocean wide.

Agents and the chandlers seen bustling back and fore;
Across the dock, the boatmen sculling with an oar.
Tugs hooted out their signals, towing craft about,
Most sailing or arriving until the tide ran out.

Time maybe for a pint or two in the old Chain Locker,
With a tattooed shipmate or local friendly docker.
Twice a day locks were manned, around high-water mark,
Pilots sent to waiting ships, ready to embark.

It wasn't just the coal cargoes that made the place well known –
A fine repair and dry dock was famous on its own.
Grain mills and a cold store stood nearby on the land,
Ammunition loaded, fire brigade on hand.

Vessels moored at anchor, from Breaksea Point to Sully,
Till summoned by the dock master, always in a hurry.
The port was home for many ships travelling blue highways,
And the best of merchant seamen in those yesterdays.

BAMSE, THE NORWEGIAN SEA DOG

He's buried in the sand dunes now – a brave sea dog of war.
A statue to this famous hound stands on the Montrose shore.
No more the old minesweeper which Bamse served time on,
Or standing on the fo'c'sle head when sailing to and from.

No more the special helmet he wore to face the Hun,
Or snarling at the enemy while standing by the gun.
No more escort duty when rounding up his crew,
Or stopping gangway entry, apart from those he knew.

No more devoted children riding on his back,
Or padding round the local shops mooching for a snack.
No more giant paw marks six foot up the wall,
Or slurping from a bowl on his own pub crawl.

No more the large fish dinners he relished every time,
Or indifference to explosions when blowing off a mine.
No more control of seamen when getting out of hand;
Just a wartime grave – a memory in the sand.

BARRY SEAMEN

Many Barry seamen, during World War Two,
Lost their lives on colliers, but hardly given due.
Mostly served as firemen down the engine room,
Along with hardy stokers and trimmers in the gloom.

In dungarees and singlets they toiled there in the heat,
Well below the waterline to a rolling beat.
They did not have much prospect, working there below,
When a U-boat shot his tin fish and set the ship aglow.

If perhaps they made it and scrambled up on deck,
Wearing gear I mentioned and sweat rag round the neck,
They faced the cold Atlantic storms or raging fires,
Perchance to gain a lifeboat afore the ship expires.

Even then, against the odds, if rescue's carried out,
Pay was stopped without delay, leaving kin with nowt.
They were unsung heroes and defence was mighty thin,
Waiting for a big bang, and plates to crumple in.

Per head of population, Barry lost the most
Of hardy merchant seamen from around our coast.
In Holton Road a monument stands for all to see –
A tribute to those brave men who sailed to keep us free.

BILL THE GUNNER

The soldier fought hostilities with bayonet and the gun –
To take a life was always thus since modern wars begun.
The airman dropped his bombs, knew not the number killed,
Sent aloft in aeroplanes where'er his bosses willed.

The sailor fired from battleships, sending men to doom,
Or delivered death by depth charge with underwater boom.
All the fighting services were trained in what they do,
Stood for king and country and all that's right and true.

Alas, the merchant seaman aboard his sitting duck
Steamed about defenceless unless he had the luck
To have an anti-aircraft gun mounted on the deck,
Perchance to hole a bomber afore it made a wreck.

Officials issued Oerlikons, a Vickers or a Bren,
Usually pretty ancient, unfamiliar to our men.
They were taught the 'hosepipe' method – in a sort of sermon –
And it wasn't very easy to shoot a flying German.

But I knew a certain captain – the skipper of a trawler –
Patrolling down the east coast, he shot 'em down to order.
As his score just mounted, the navy mused "How high?"
For when the foe approached him, he shot 'em out the sky.

He was pressed to give a lecture before the convoy started off,
To a bunch of gunner ratings and a Royal Navy toff.
The skipper wasn't quite prepared as he rolled in through the door,
So said he'd answer questions from that lot on the floor.

It was the ribboned admiral who spoke and said like this:
"Skipper, pray, please tell us of how you rarely miss."
"'Tis easy," said the master. "We don't fret at all.
I send to get my mate out – he's a man wot likes a brawl.

"'There's another coming, Bill,' I sez. 'Go shoot the bugger down.'
So he ups and mans 'is Oerlikons with concentrated frown,
Cos he tends to wait a bit till he sees the pilot guys,
Then 'e sprays 'em in the cockpit – an' right between the eyes.

"That's the one that gets 'em, 'an puts 'em off their stroke.
They nosedive to the water in a cloud of spray and smoke.
I winks at Bill and throws the chalk – so 'e can keep a tally,
And mark the ones we've blown up, an' sunk there in Bomb Alley."

BILL

One thousand miles from nowhere, a tin fish hit its mark.
Its target was a British ship which foundered in the dark.
The crew were killed or injured and could not stay afloat –
Just four of them were able to make it to a boat.

They watched their ship go down upon a Christmas Eve,
In a state of shock pondering their reprieve.
There they stayed and suffered – in tropic heat they sweltered.
Death was standing by them – no comfort and unsheltered.

They finished all the bully beef and licked the milk cans dry.
One of them had died by now as forty days went by.
The remaining three were skeletons – living, just, but weak.
When picked up by the navy could not stand or speak.

Three weeks on, saw them home – recovered bit by bit,
Replacing all their papers and merchant seaman's kit.
One man was a mate of mine – let's just call him Bill.
I'd met him there when rescued and very, very ill.

I thought I'd go and see him – take him to a pub.
Found his home in Liverpool, and thereby lies the rub.
I knocked the door – his wife came out, told me that her Bill,
Bored with life ashore, refused to bide there still.

Ten days only he was home – then he said to me,
"I'm signing on again, old girl," and went off back to sea.

Derived from a story told on the radio in one of the ever memorable
Postscript*s narrated after the BBC news during 1941 by Frank
Laskier – from his book of transcripts:* My Name Is Frank.

BATTERY POINT

On Battery Point at Portishead there's a slab of Portland stone.
It's there in dedication, standing proud alone,
To seamen of the West Country who sailed here close to shore,
On voyages of history in times of peace and war.

These sterling men of England cast off from local quays,
Roved to far-flung countries across the seven seas.
Outward-bound they passed this spot over sands of time,
Battened down, Bristol-style, vessels in their prime.

They went to join the convoys with danger at the fore,
Or missions of discovery when sent out to explore,
Flew the old red ensign wherever they were going,
Kept our lifelines open and the commerce flowing.

Whatever type of venture saw them far from home,
They had to deal with elements across the mighty foam.
Hail now to our mariners going west across the bay;
The Portland stone awaits – on your return one day.

BIRNBECK IS A LADY

This island rock stands alone;
Empty buildings – no one's home.
Pity then the awful waste,
Like a lady too darn chaste.

Come, my friends – court her dearly,
Build esteem, bedeck her clearly,
Nurture her; she'll glow and shine,
Beauty growing most sublime.

Such a phoenix from the ashes,
All-embracing to the masses,
Along her pier, beloved, waiting,
Weston's jewel – scintillating.

BIRNBECK ISLAND PIER

This ancient rock still proudly stands
Midst ebb and flow by Weston Sands.
In its heyday host to steamers,
Calling here decked out with streamers.

Entertainment – high spring tides,
Victorian evenings, lots besides.
Now, my friends, this is the story –
We'd like it back to former glory.

Connected to the land by pier,
'Tis been unused for many a year,
Except for answering mayday's flare,
Brave men launching lifeboats there.

Let us too respond to calls,
Encourage life around its walls,
Give it heart and pulse anew,
Then stroll the pier – it's good for you.

BOB'S WAR

Bob Bromley sailed the savage seas all throughout the war,
Suffered fraught conditions and told me what he saw.
His first ship was a tanker – the MV *James Maguire*,
From which he saw the *Jervis Bay* and *San Demetrio* on fire.

Fired upon quite ruthlessly by the raider Admiral Scheer,
Totting up huge losses in that 1940 year,
He served aboard the *Robert Hands* then the *Empire Oil*,
Till torpedoed in the engine room and sunk amid turmoil.

A victim of a U-boat and her noxious ploy,
Bob made it to a lifeboat till rescued by *St Croix*,
(She was a Canadian warship – took him to St John,
This destroyer reaching there, September '41).

(It was the gallant *Ottawa* plucked more men from the sea.
Bob's crew mates were injured, but there was no guarantee. . . .
So grateful to be picked up, on that fated trip,
Only then be sunk again when a tin fish struck the ship.)

Housed in a wooden building, the windows clad by wire,
It looked a certain deathtrap if overrun by fire,
(Very soon it was – killed three-fifty men;
There is a special monument erected there to them.)

Then passage on a steamer, a ship named *Caribou* –
Running down the east coast with all her lights on view.
Bob was apprehensive by this heedless glow,
With 600 passengers packed there tight below.

Again our Bob was lucky – made Halifax all right,
But the *Caribou* weeks later was blown to hell at night,
With heavy loss of life, many children drowned as well,
Mostly wives and family of service personnel.

Bob then crossed the Rockies – a five-day train ordeal –
Until he reached Vancouver and signed aboard *Fort Steel*,
In due course arriving home until the next convoy,
Then went and joined another ship, the SS *Iroquois*.

Two years on the *Harper* sailing round the world,
A brief spell on the *Waldon Hill* as Bob's young life unfurled,
Till at last the *Chesapeake* in October '45;
Paying off in '46, our Bob remained alive.

It's a privilege to know old Bob and count him as a friend –
A dauntless British seaman, who stayed there till the end.

CALLED OUT

Early morning Christmas Eve – preparing for the day.
"Ho ho," said old Cory's, "you have to go away.
There's a ship out there in trouble and the weather's pretty vile –
A Dutchman's lost his rudder and the Captain's lost his smile."

Six good men were called up, and hauled away from bed.
We rushed and manned the *Portgarth* up and sailed just on the ebb,
Steaming west at a rate of knots and baro' falling fast,
Southerly gale upon the beam and spray above the mast.

MV *Harns* off Hartland Point, begging for a tow;
Portgarth rolling wildly and seventy miles to go.
Two thousand tons of cargo ship and a load of steel as well,
Wallowing there ahead of us, hiding in the swell.

Horseshoe Rocks abeam now, and our quarry is in sight,
Riding to the weather and in a sorry plight.
Contact made on VHF and coastguard told the story:
Making fast in storm-force 10 and the wind in constant fury.

Risking lives or broken limbs, the chance we had to take –
Get her home for Christmas, lads, or the holiday's at stake.
With hearts in mouths and lifebelts on we have our just reward –
She takes a lurch and throws us all, but we have a line aboard.

We pay out our wire and turn her round, and head on east by south.
Bit by bit we're winning now into the channel's mouth.
Wind and tide on quarter as the tow takes on a sheer –
A tugman's hell, but we're losing swell as the Devon coast draws near.

The job still fraught, the line comes taut as we run the easting down.
All looks well, but it's hard to tell as nightfall brings a frown.
Three hours to flow, high spring tide and a storm-force wind on hand;
Hazards ahead: One Fathom Bank and the dangerous Culver Sand.

Disaster strikes: the wire parts. "Captain, anchor down."
MV *Harns* is safe for now, at East Culver holding ground.
Portgarth's gear is all a mess with spring jammed off the drum;
The forward winch as well kaput – it's what the weather's done.

Head south now – Blue Anchor Roads, so we may work on deck,
Sheltered from the worst of it, but hailstones down our neck.
It's Christmas morn and we are sworn to bring this coaster in –
Repair the wire and return to it – we are going to win.

Made fast again as daylight comes, we surely have her now,
But the cable cuts as the lead just rips and slices on her bow.
A tug came out of Cardiff with the Welshman's dauntless crew –
They also had a line aboard, but parted two by two.

Another tug from Newport passed a brand-new spring,
Yet again we parted with a now familiar ring.
Then they sent *Point Gilbert* down – dancing all the way.
Still atrocious weather on this our Christmas Day.

Sorted out our for'd winch and we'd spliced the line up tight,
Also mended fax machine and the phone now works all right.
The *Gilbert* took hold forward, well and truly fast,
Portgarth with a bridle aft and on our way at last.

The *Hallgarth* out from Cardiff to help us to deliver,
Heading up to Newport to aid us up the river.
Things were pretty fraught again as we cleared the Middle Banks,
And problems near the bell buoy as we start to give our thanks.

Our quarter line in the Dutchman's screw as he worked a touch astern;
We cut it off and shortened up – put another out in turn.
The *Gilbert* sniffed the bottom, which didn't help at all,
But the bow was towed from danger by the action of the *Hall*.

Eventually we moored her up – it was almost Boxing Day.
Over forty hours without our sleep, the lads have earned their pay.
The moral of this story – if you want your Christmas pud –
Is never lose your rudder, or change your livelihood!

CAPE HORN: THE VOYAGE OF THE *FLORENCE*

I love to hear of windjammers sailing round the Horn,
Of iron men and wooden ships, billowed canvas worn,
The roaring of the forties, hardened bucko mates,
Of flying fish, albacore, and salt beef on the plates.

One ship was the *Florence* – an ocean-going hound,
Thirty men aboard her, San Francisco-bound.
This old but sturdy vessel cast off on the tide –
Coal was loaded earlier from further up the Clyde.

A motley bunch made up the 'crowd' plus a 'pier-head jump'.
'Schooner-rigged' were most of 'em, but all could man the pump.
It was not for the wages they signed on as a crew,
But for dogged British seamen the only trade they knew.

A hard life, then, for officers and men before the mast,
Fighting nature's elements round their world so vast.
A five-month haul to Frisco by the wind's own power,
Watch and watch unless called out, bell struck on the hour.

Some weeks of the voyage were in part sublime,
Weather fair and holding by equator's line,
Brilliant stars above 'em, Jupiter at dawn,
Overhauling heavy gear ready for the Horn.

Swapping yarns in dog watches while puffing on a pipe,
Gently swaying mastheads pointing at the night.
Tranquil days of sailor work – barefoot days were here –
With spectre of the southern climes as the Cape drew near.

Soon they met the greybeards, the fury and the sound,
Thundering seas unfettered that went the globe around.
These towering seas against them with a slant upon a sail,
Trying to beat to windward under squalls of hail.

Weeks and weeks it took them, fighting hard in awe,
Doubling back and crossing the courses held before.
Eventually a friendly wind helped them full and by –
A north-west course now possible beneath a leaden sky.

Swaying on the foot ropes, an AB took a clout,
Stretching for the canvas when it bellowed out,
Falling from the jackstay when struck by threshing sails,
Dead before the water, he hit topgallant rails.

They couldn't go to find him by launching of a boat,
For the chances of retrieval were risky and remote.
The hands were getting weary now and longing for the shore –
Work was very tedious and plenty more in store.

"Just think a bit", I says to me, to check upon a notion,
"Of what it meant to deep-sea men a long time on the ocean,
Subject to a discipline hard to find ashore,
Rations poor and meagre but always wanting more."

Rusty-red fresh water sloshing in the tanks –
Portioned was the last of it, so thirsty in the ranks.
Discussions turned to fisticuffs while captive there at sea –
The breaking of monotony seeks different scenery.

A Yankee silver dollar hammered to the mast:
The prize for any lookout that spied the land at last.
A good excuse to lay aloft to rest the salt-cased brain,
Raising of the spirits and easing of the pain.

Till a shout of "Fire" went up – the cargo was alight,
Finding it deep-seated, smouldering day and night.
Soon was made a landfall just thirty miles away
From their destination in foggy Frisco Bay.

The fire was doused while anchored, then a berth secured
Among the many sailing ships that hove in from abroad.
There in San Francisco – that place of booze an' pimps –
Several crew were lost to drink and hijacked by the crimps.

Cargo was discharged there and holds cleaned up for grain –
Port Costa was the loading berth – then set off home again.
"All's well," seamen shout as sailing to the south,
Heading for the Horn again and the roaring forties' mouth.

Wind stubborn from the north-west, it blew a howling gale –
Hotfooting then before it with just a foretopsail.
Wings enough for the strength of it, now blowing up a storm.
Not one could stand on the reeling hull; damage was the norm.

Then a lull and fog came in, the *Florence* struck the ice,
Bowsprit smashed and hull stove in – happened in a trice.
Making best they could of it, by the sun's dim light
Set a course to Falkland's Isles to put the damage right.

Hiring men and riveters, the *Florence* then made good –
Spars culled from a previous wreck fashioned there from wood.
The hulk of Brunel's *Great Britain* beached across the bay –
Part of Stanley's scenery before they sailed away.

The doldrums brought the blazing sun though sometimes it rained;
Ten days of calm or few light airs – nothing much was gained.
"More blooming days, more dollars," one of the seamen grinned.
Small comfort to the old man, who whistled for the wind.

Later on they made their way, vessel running free,
Approaching then the Cornish coast and a greying sea
Through the wreaths of fog, lookouts at their posts,
Falmouth-bound for orders further round the coast.

Provisioned once again, then sent to Ireland's shore –
Discharging port was Sligo, then swept the holds once more.
Eventually in Glasgow, hands required their pay
For their work on *Florence* while sixteen months away.

For the ancient mariner, now watchman on the ship,
A time of calm nostalgia afore she sails next trip.
The mainmast and the rigging are quiet among the spars
Until she comes to life again and rolls them at the stars.

BURIED AT SEA

A vessel stops for a shortish spell,
Rolling easy on the ocean swell,
Ensign lowered to half mast,
Burial party standing fast.

Our deceased is canvas-clad,
A stitched-up nose the last to add.
Weights are coupled round his feet,
Confirming passage to the deep.

A solemn crew are sure to muster
Around a hatch board and red duster.
The Captain reads a final word;
A body's launched undeterred.

An entry made in official log;
Full ahead the engines flog.
The deed is done on a distant wave –
A seaman's gone to a deep-sea grave.

Buried at sea – or interred –
No other name is easy heard.
Not burnt to ashes or Boot Hill –
Davy's locker takes them still.

CAPTAIN NORTH OF THE *ATLANTIC CONVEYOR*

Captain Ian North, when he was called to war,
Epitomised the spirit of merchant-navy lore.
Resourceful with ability and a bushy beard,
Showing calm authority, he was well revered.

His ship was berthed in Liverpool when his orders came
To steam down to the Falklands and help refute the claim.
He then prepared his vessel into a breed of carrier,
Converted for the choppers and the vital Harrier.

Laden with Chinooks, Wessex and the Lynx,
The Captain's innovation ironed out many kinks.
Stores and apparatus loaded to complete –
Staggering in so short a time, and quite a marvellous feat.

Steaming with the battle group, they went to do their bit;
Later, near San Carlos, she took a bomber's hit,
Spreading fire and mayhem caused by Exocet,
Reaching fuel in army trucks standing by on deck.

The sinking of *Conveyor* was a bona fide disaster:
Twelve men gave their lives inclusive of her master.
Essentially civilians, they didn't have to go,
But steadfast British mariners never would say no.

They went to serve our country as seamen always will,
Crucial to the campaign with their special skill.
Flying our red duster his crew were going forth,
Under fine tradition – and Captain Ian North.

CAPTAIN F. J. "JOHNNIE" WALKER, CB, DSO, RN

Captain Johnnie Walker of wartime history
Rates so very highly in annals of the sea.
His personal contribution to survival of convoys
Was demanding and immense to our merchant-navy boys.

He was the brain and sinew of our escort groups,
The training and the triumph of corvettes and the sloops.
He switched a shepherd's role from defensive to attack
By chasing hard the submarines prowling in a pack.

Sailing into battle with speakers blaring loud,
'A-hunting We Will Go' playing to the crowd,
Ordering his signalman to hoist 'The General Chase',
Sounding out the enemy, pursuing them at pace.

Relentless were his tactics, depth-charging day and night,
Illuminating enemies to hinder fight or flight.
U-boats had a problem then – 'twas hard to find a way
To stalk their prey of merchant ships being kept at bay.

Gradually the upper hand was gained by Captain Walker,
Convincing too our bombers to stretch across the water.
Sadly though it took its toll in 1944 –
He died worn out with stress of work by that cruel sea war.

Remember, many seamen lost their lives throughout,
Torpedoed in the ocean and scuppered by the Kraut.
His system persevered though, and helped to clear the way
To purge the sea of U-boats for the landings at D-Day.

His life was dedicated to destruction of the foe,
To the service of his country and evil overthrow.
He was a naval hero when times were desperate grim –
Britain ruled the waves again with captains such as him.

CONVOY TM1

Nine tankers in a convoy in 1942
Steamed from Port of Spain, each with valiant crew,
Sailing to Gibraltar to feed the Allied needs,
Hampered by a headwind reducing modest speeds.

A U-boat close at hand reported back to base,
So Dönitz gathered wolf packs and sent them on apace
To stalk the lumbering vessels laden down with oil,
And sink them with torpedoes by their toxic toil.

The convoy had an escort – a destroyer and corvettes –
But failed to stop the enemy discern the silhouettes.
First the *British Vigilance* was hammered in the dark –
She dropped back through the convoy derelict and stark.

Albert Ellsworth then blew up while leading column one;
Within a couple of minutes, she was entirely gone.
Next *Oltenia Two* was struck – very soon thereafter –
Then *Minister Wedel* and *Norvik*, totting up disaster.

The escorts tried so hard to defend the scene,
But those infernal U-boats foiled the navy screen.
Empire Lytton's tanks were breached – set the sea on fire.
Next day *British Dominion* was turned into a pyre.

Only two ships made it to Gibraltar's welcome berth.
Our tenacious seamen showed their dauntless worth
By shipping out regardless against a deadly foe,
Knowing they were sitting ducks travelling in a row.

(Only Cliona *and the* Vanja *survived from the nine tankers in
Convoy TM1 – arriving on 14 January 1943. Two U-boats were
damaged during the attacks.)*

CONVOYS (1)

Our lads that sailed in convoys – officers and ranks –
Deserve a special mention and our heartfelt thanks.
Most vessels were quite sound – manned by crews well trained;
Others were the opposite, most scrap and rusty-stained.

These doughty merchant seamen knew their cruel fate
When struck by cunning sea wolves lurking there in wait.
If they lived to tell the story and strived to stay afloat,
They struggled then with hardships aboard an open boat.

Still they served our country, sailing there and back,
Hauling vital cargoes in times that looked so black.
A dangerous job in peacetime, they continued just the same
During war at sea, my friends – through the shock and flame.

'Course it was the ammo ships that were blown to smithereens
While plodding past the periscopes of hidden submarines.
Also, on the tankers one hardly had a chance
When spotted by the enemy rearmed out of France.

The mines were pretty lethal, lurking God knows where,
Happen chance to strike one – turmoil then and there.
The bombers stretched to reach 'em had a bit of fun,
Dropping tons of dynamite against a paltry gun.

Then there was the weather, with storm and hurricanes –
Very near impossible to steer intended lanes,
Especially wild Atlantic and freezing Russian run;
Casualties horrendous till the job was done.

There was a school of thought – to foil the U-boat ace,
Just give the Royal Air Force some extra fuel space,
In long-range Liberators to patrol as ocean scout,
Instead of burning cities and knocking civvies out.

Later on this was done – though several months too late,
Condemning many cargo ships with their precious freight.
Gradually the sinkings were cut by lessons learned,
Though still appalling losses until the tide was turned.

So crucial were these convoys to the war by land and air,
There's a mighty debt to seamen that served for us out there.
They paid the price of liberty by standing firm and fast,
And still we fly their ensign – stubborn from the mast.

CONVOYS (2)

The convoy steamed on its ocean ride,
A grey wolf pack lurked astride.
Explosions then lit up the dark –
Torpedoes struck their helpless mark.

Naval escorts chased around,
Contacts made with echo sound.
Need to catch the U-boats there
In vast and deep hidden lair.

Fires and screams mid lowered boats,
Burning oil and carley floats.
Urgent freight will not get through;
Nor would many shipwrecked crew.

Some ships scatter on their own,
Others sinking in the foam.
Daylight comes to count the cost –
Men that died and tonnage lost.

Depth-charge bombs still booming aft,
Flotsam left of burning craft –
Another night of helpless slaughter,
Of brave seamen on the water.

This the way they fought their war,
Reluctant heroes at the fore.
Six long years they sailed and bled
Under ensigns white and red.

CORY'S MEN

Cory's have a fleet of tugs, their funnels gleaming red.
They tow all kinds of craft about, and sometimes push instead.
There's Z-Pellers and tractors – single-screw as well.
Its cool to watch them 'bone in mouth' steaming through the swell.

When ready there and waiting to aid all kinds of ships,
We carry out our maintenance when they're just radar blips,
Standing by to do our job, with mobile phone and bleepers,
Stemming there with pent-up power to tow those ocean creepers.

Sometimes we go a long way; oft-times it's just a dap.
Every job is different, and we can handle that,
Cos we ply our trade at night or day where the hungry seagulls fuss –
All weathers too, especially wind, when the worried captains cuss.

Underneath the bows we go – where things may get so dicey.
Oh, how we yearn for a modern tug (but Cory's say they're pricey)!
Get on with it and pass a line – we cannot blame our tools.
A foreign crew, its our hard luck – they don't know the rules.

A puff of smoke, a bit of weight, we bend 'em round the pier.
"Nice job," the pilot says as we retrieve our gear.
Rack 'em, pack 'em, and stack 'em – this is what we say.
Leave it up to Cory's men – the tugs are on the way.

D –DAY, 6 JUNE 1944

I went to view the battlefields of Operation Overlord –
Fifty miles of coastline from Utah Beach to Sword.
To gain a hold in Normandy, D-Day was the key –
A step to free all Europe and beat Hitler's Germany.

We marshalled all our forces after well-honed drills,
Comprising all resources with their special skills.
Twelve thousand Allied airplanes, three million men and more,
Land and sea and airmen determined to endure.

A convoy of 6,000 steamed across the sea,
From warships to assault craft, burgees flying free.
While our paratroopers jumped to hold the flanks,
Heavy naval gunfire supported all the ranks.

Resistance here was mighty strong through the hostile surf –
They fought and strived side by side to gain the foreign turf.
There are many tales of bravery and yarns of derring-do,
Bad luck or just good fortune – plus error factors too.

Steaming through old minefields, making life quite fraught,
Mulberries were towed across to make a discharge port,
For berthing of the Liberty ships – seven at a time –
While Operation Pluto was the laying of pipeline.

The planning and arranging, a monumental slog;
This final push to victory, a mortal heavy job.
Supplies proceeding quickly – another fine endeavour –
Though there was a setback provided by the weather.

This Normandy invasion was the biggest undertaken,
Embarked upon with Allies, confidence unshaken.
I paid respect with colleagues at the wonder of the plan,
And the acts of courage displayed by every man.

Paid homage in the graveyards as I took my tribute strolls,
Faced the plaque at Arromanches for merchant-navy souls.
We will not forget them – history points the truth:
On the altar of our freedom brave men gave their youth.

DAVY JONES'S LOCKER

I have sailed on mighty oceans and many a dangerous bay,
With Davy Jones a-calling, inviting me to stay.
I thought then of his locker and contents of his deck –
Countless ships throughout the years sunk or made a wreck.

Fishing boats and tankers, missing submarines,
Once overloaded ferries and ancient quinquiremes,
Warships and the liners, planes without their floats,
Kon-Tiki rafts and whalers and fancy motor boats.

Vessels deeply laden that never reached their goal,
Strewn across the murky wastes with ghostly silent soul;
The masts and yards of sailing ships pointing stiff and stark,
No use now to anyone, static in the dark.

Golden coins and cannonades, part of pirates' treasure,
Baubles from a Spanish chest sunken there forever,
Untold tombs of mariners and those that took a dip,
And many rusty anchors from craft that had to slip.

Cannonballs, gun barrels, bells made out of brass,
Dinner plates of sailors and portholes' rounded glass.
Wood has rotted slowly in places that we know,
Barnacles encrusting on iron there below.

The fishes keep them company, the massive whale and shark,
Giant squid and serpents, lurking in the dark.
I thought I'd turn his offer down – that Davy made to me –
Endeavour now to keep afloat on Neptune's fickle sea.

DEDICATION

Imagine you are on Welsh Back and picture, if you can,
Attending our memorial unveiled by Princess Anne.
With her royal pennant flying there supreme,
A joyful day in every way, the climax of a dream.
Leaning on the railings, a waving Bristol crowd;
The regal standardbearers, smart and mighty proud;
Sea cadets and school kids, boy marines as well,
Officials in their finery and policemen from Bridewell.

All mustered here together, upon this cobbled strand,
'For Those in Peril on the Sea' by Salvation Army band,
The *Matthew* moored alongside in a handy spot,
Atop the poop a cannoneer set to fire a shot.
Invited guests and veterans all are standing fast,
With the duty bugler stationed by the mast.
A welcome said and prayers are read – our Padre at the scene –
Dedication carried out by the city dean.

The Princess lays a floral wreath fashioned as an anchor.
With kind words she sallies forth – our chairman duly thanks her.
Chatting on and running late she tarries neath the trees,
When introduced to mariners who'd sailed the seven seas.
They spoke of U-boat actions in the war against the foe,
The sinkings and endurance which only they could know.
So there you have the picture as the public turns away,
Leaving thirsty shellbacks and those who forged our day.

They knew the satisfaction at the last post's final sound,
On completion of their monument now on hallowed ground.
When I regard this tribute, invariably I find
Thoughts of merchant seamen – their deaths invade my mind.
Perhaps it is sometime ago and the misery has gone,
But it seems to me while we're alive we cannot bid, "So long."
That's why, shipmate, it's not too late (and not only in November)
To shed a tear while viewing here and say "*We will remember.*"

*On the unveiling of the Merchant Navy Memorial at Welsh Back,
Bristol, May 2000.*

DEFENSIVELY EQUIPPED MERCHANT SHIPS (DEMS)

(The Arming of Merchant Ships in WWII: The DEMS Gunners)

They sailed aboard our merchant ships and manned outdated guns
To defend against our enemies: Italians and the Huns.
They were gunners from the army or navy volunteers –
The rattle of the ack-ack was music to their ears.

Seaports kept artillery from the war before,
Handy now to give each ship to guard a little more.
Usually a Lewis gun they went and cheerfully manned,
But always took a hammer as it often stuck or jammed.

During those hostilities while trying not to drown,
Using Oerlikons or Bofors to shoot the shells around,
They angled high for bombers that gave 'em such concern,
Most likely from a four-inch gun perched there at the stern.

Twelve-pounders were the norm, set upon the bow –
That would be a three-inch shell, describing it just now.
They were standing by to shoot every minute of the hour,
In case a deadly U-boat showed its conning tower.

Mounted on the bridge wing, the fo'c'sle or the poop,
Ready for the action when bombers came to swoop,
They fired away at anything threatening with a will,
Showing loads of courage and not a lack of skill.

The two-man crews were legendary in annals of the sea,
Included in with seamen when naming pedigree.
They couldn't stop torpedoes submarines would send,
But mostly those brave gunners stayed there till the end.

Dedicated to Ted Thomas, DEMS gunner, Bristol MNA.

FISHING

My mate and I go angling – we go hunting for the trout.
It's on the way to Nailsea – my mate gives me a shout.
We pack our high-tech carbon rods and half a case of stout,
Then off we go just fishing, when there's no work about.

We park along by Harry's hut and pay a small deposit,
Stroll up by the grassy cut and lay our gear upon it.
The wind behind of the wintry kind, we eye the rainy skies;
Weatherproof and eager now, we bend on the fancy flies.

We point our rods at the rainbow foe and cast our coloured lines,
Forget hard times and look for signs of where the fishes go.
We get in trim and haul them in at a satisfactory rate.
I tell my friend, "You'll have to spend – did you bring your chequebook,
mate?"

With a dirty grin and a mighty swing, he casts for one last time.
He's in a state cos he's just caught eight, an' he don't think much of mine.
But the job is done, we've had some fun, we're heading now to pay,
But never mind cos we did find 'twas a brilliant angling day.

We gut our catch in a nice clean sink and go without delay
To the local pub to talk of fish an' the one that got away.
My mate and me went boozing – we drank till they chucked us out.
A great sport is the tippling – after chasing the rainbow trout.

1996

FROM A RUSSIAN CONVOY

A cargo ship is steaming into the Barents Sea,
Heaving, rolling, pitching, bound for Murmansk Quay.
The previous night, in awful plight, her convoy had been scattered –
Best-laid plans are history now as slim defence is shattered.

Arctic storms are frequent, floating mines abound,
Dodgy is the compass and ice floes all around.
Watching out for U-boats and torpedoes' mortal run,
The only means of fighting, an antiquated gun.

The fog and snow – sixty below in the freezing winds!
Sodden clothes and eyes are froze staring through the bins.
High on deck, lifelines rigged to struggle fore and aft,
Shipping seas all over in deeply laden draught.

Through a gap a spotter plane at distance overhead,
Homing in the Stukas with spectre of bloodshed.
Vital cargo must get through – vehicles and tanks,
Ammo with the aircraft and stores for army ranks.

Seldom war quite like it in all our history,
Knowing that our chances are only two from three.
Even berthed in Russia, the bombs fall every day.
Twenty minutes' flying time – the Germans have their way.

There is no special thanks for this appalling run,
Facing awful weather and unremitting Hun.
Many merchant seamen never make it through,
Giving all for country in this year of '42.

HMS *SNAEFELL*

(Previously Named PS *Barry*, also PS *Waverley*,
Launched, 1907; Sunk, 1941; Rediscovered, 2010)

There was a team of divers that found a sunken wreck
Eight miles away from Sunderland on the North Sea deck.
It was the sweeper *Snaefell* – all trace lost till now,
Since bombed and sunk in '41 by damage to her bow.

She was launched as PS *Barry* when built so long ago –
A well-loved paddle steamer scheduled to and fro.
Her glossy shining paintwork was red and pearly white,
Her bunting and the ensign on halyards whipping tight.

She gave so many people a time of bracing pleasure,
Merrymaking passengers enjoying days to treasure.
Registered in South Wales in her early years,
Calling at the channel ports to cheering from the piers.

Outstanding in the Great War for aquatic chores,
Transporting at Gallipoli many men and stores –
Dodging mines and shells in the Dardanelles Campaign
Earned this speedy lady everlasting fame.

Later on in '26 she steamed our southern climes,
Sailing out of Brighton and Hastings many times.
There she was the *Waverley* – famous just the same,
Till the second war arrived and changed her name again.

She then became the *Snaefell*, minesweeping for the navy,
  Paintwork now a drab grey and daubed a sort of wavy.
When called again she answered with urgent crucial work,
  Withdrawing many troops from the beaches at Dunkirk.

True, our hardy mariners steered her through the rough,
  Kept the old girl going when the going was so tough.
Like other paddle steamers that thrust ahead with pride,
A mortal wound, her time was up – she crossed the bar and died.

Her paddles rest in mud and murk, but once stirred up the foam,
  Her binnacle of dented brass no more a compass home.
Her long sharp bow is mangled iron, the engine room a tomb –
Alas, the fate of *Snaefell* when a German bomb went 'boom'!

GATHERED HERE

Once again gathered here, we count the cost and flow
Of those that crossed the bar – the men we used to know.
Although perhaps we shed a tear at setting of their sun,
Let's celebrate the life they led – a voyage home now run.

In battles lost with foe, or ancient year's last mile,
It's how a life was lived that makes a man worthwhile.
Those that went sometime ago we remember still,
Upholding debt of gratitude, boding no one ill.

Others gone more recently our grief we now defend,
A legacy astern – for nought goes with us in the end.
For each of us our day will come, and then our God may say,
"Welcome, shellback. Come aboard – your friends are left to pray."

HARRY'S MEDALS

Harry needs some medals – he was told off by the Duke;
Also from the Princess he earned a slight rebuke.
But Harry still ain't got 'em – he hasn't made a claim.
How and where to get them? To help him is my aim.

He could make them out of bottle tops – they would look quite snazzy –
Or cut a bit of cardboard box and turn them out quite jazzy.
He could drill a hole in a two-bob bit, or perhaps a half a crown,
Or else a copper penny if he likes that shade of brown.

He could use the plug from out the kitchen sink,
But if it's made of rubber it wouldn't really clink;
So perhaps a crafty one, like a Yankee dollar;
Failing that, the battered disc from off the old dog's collar.

He could use some silver paper just to make 'em shine,
Or a bit of coloured plastic – that would look quite fine.
It's possible to find some wood and whittle it around,
And chisel at the edges to make a nice surround.

Then find a strip of ribbon that has a bit of stripe,
Especially if it's vertical – I think you know the type.
Fasten it securely by a length of wire,
Pin it on his blazer, stand back and admire.

Then when the Bristol public asks, "What's all they for?"
Tongue-in-cheek our Harry says, "I won 'em in the war."
'Course there is another method, the one I like the most:
Just fill the bloody forms in and have 'em sent by post!

September 2001

I AM NO SAILOR

The crew are just fine on their ship of the line,
Rolling and pitching in seas,
While making headway in salty blown spray
I'm retching on hands and my knees.

She's sheering and shaking as homeward she's making,
Taking it all in her stride,
While I'm in the bog, as sick as a dog,
Regretting this nautical ride.

I'm the colour of green in a bouncing latrine,
My eyes all streaming and red.
There is a long way to go – I'd rather not know
As I puke and wish I was dead.

I SAW THE FLYING DUTCHMAN

I'll not forget the fright from that November night
When I saw the *Flying Dutchman* sailing past.
I will remember, son, till I'm sent to kingdom come,
The canvas on her yards and ancient mast.

She had a starboard list in a silver mist,
Dead silent was her passage overall.
The sails were full and blooming, an ashen light was looming,
No wind nor moon were thereabouts at all.

If you were asking me, I was privileged to see
A ghostly apparition sent abroad.
You may raise an eyebrow hair, but I was surely there,
An' I'll swear it on the Bible of Our Lord.

I'D LOVE TO SAIL ON A TRAMP AGAIN

I would love to sail on a tramp again on a voyage north to south,
Steaming off to warmer climes from ports like Avonmouth,
Perhaps to stand as lookout on a lonely fo'c'sle head,
A weather eye for other craft with sidelights green and red.

Warm enough for comfort on a balmy night,
In seaman's gear of tee shirt, bleached in cotton white,
A faded pair of dungarees – well-scrubbed old blue jeans –
On my feet the moccasins I'd bought in New Orleans.

I'd love to keep a watch again on a gently pitching ship –
Nothing else for miles around on a foreign-going trip.
The brilliant stars on a dark night humbling to the soul –
A freedom known to seamen bracing with the roll.

The sea is always there and always will remain,
Though my life has been – so cannot go again.
I will sail the world once more, conversely, as it seems,
Pacing on a lonely deck – only in my dreams.

INJUSTICE

I feel for the men who have been cheated –
The ones that went through the war.
They fought for the process of freedom
And saw all the blood and the gore.
They are strapped with a measly old pension,
Though they rarely complain;
Their pleasure is down at the local
In out of the wind and the rain.
Say "Good day" to the landlord
And just settle down with a jar,
Tamp on a pipe of tobacco,
Relax and smoke in the bar.

Now those bloody do-gooders
Have ruined the peace of the old
By making them stop what they are doing
And go out for a smoke in the cold.
I reckon for all them true smokers
That laid their life on the line
It's a case of selfish injustice
And law ahead of its time.
The heroes of England, like Nelson,
Would turn and revolve in their tombs
If they heard of the rule of no smoking –
An insult added to wounds.

MERCHANT SEAMEN

'In war and peace they plied their trade
Over the angry seas
Remember them as here you stand
Beneath these placid trees.'

Inscription on the Merchant Navy Memorial, Welsh Back, Bristol.

INSPIRATION

How often have I started out, no verses in my head?
Perhaps while eating breakfast, or buttering my bread,
Then something will occur to me, though maybe lacking glamour,
So toil to set the rhyme out, and probably the grammar.
Consulting of the dictionary, try to sort the tenses,
Shape it all about a bit – appeal it to the senses.

But now and then, while boozing,
Words don't need such choosing.
My poem then – so refined –
Sits perfect, healthy in my mind.

But then next day it comes to nought –
I've disremembered every thought . . .

When I'm sober.

JOHN'S VOYAGE

My brother John's a seaman and once he said to me,
"I'll tell you of a voyage in my early days at sea.
The ship was the *Consuelo* – in '46, I'm sure,
I was a young apprentice and relatively pure.

"The Continent was starving – the people needed grain,
So we went to fetch a cargo from Canada's domain.
Sailing from the Humber and through the Pentland Firth,
Fifteen knots on Yorkshire coal the engines showed their worth.

"Heading north of west on that hot midsummer's day,
Making for old Montreal, just eight long days away.
The weather was so perfect – horizon very clear –
Earning pay while on the way as Belle Isle Straits drew near.

"In time we raised Newfoundland, her coasts on either side.
Chancing fog and icebergs, went on our risky ride.
Of course we had no radar then, but steamed on through the night;
Came tomorrow morning – what a marvellous sight!

"The straits are frozen over for six months of the year,
But this June day the fish could play and whales were basking here.
Sunlight off the growlers when my trick at the wheel,
Accompanied by herring gulls and green-winged Arctic teal.

"Close to the Long Range Mountains, with snow up to the peaks,
We could see the polar bears fishing in the creeks;
Also spied the white fox straying from its lair,
Encouraged by the temperature warming up the air.

"There were several sightings of caribou and moose
Midst ever changing colours and trees of mighty spruce.
Taking in the scenery while running with the tide,
The view was truly awesome – my eyes were open wide.

"Towards the Gulf of Lawrence, through the Straits of Labrador,
No other craft were thereabouts, but porpoises galore.
I was so very fortunate to see nature at its best –
Even hardy seamen were visibly impressed.

"I thought that I must tell you of this voyage of delight –
The beauty of these latitudes from morn till fading light.
Wish everyone could see it – make believers of us all,
If aboard an ocean freighter from Hull to Montreal."

JOHN'S DAILY WALK

I step out every morning down a country lane,
Spy the little birds, the moorhens and the crane,
Perhaps a climbing squirrel or lazy grazing horse,
While ambling round the village on my observant course.

I often spot a seagull gliding low across the land;
This takes me back across the years – seamen understand
I may recall of earlier times when down the River Plate,
Or when I was a tanker man sailing off Kuwait,

Steaming down to Rio and Recife on the way,
Surfing roaring forties and round to Botany Bay,
Suzy San in Kobe, where I spent some time,
Warmer climes of weather an' crossing of the line.

I think of all those ladies that were so cute to me –
Departing sad, but keen to go when I returned to sea.
I sit down for a breather, and watch the mums' school run,
Thrusting buttocks, pushing prams – to this old man it's fun.

I arrive back home again, my walking voyage over,
Daydreaming of my early days as a seaman rover.
But still I have that feeling – that latent, blatant urge –
To sail away to sea again, the landlocked air to purge.

Thoughts from my brother John while out walking.

LIFEBOATS

Many thousand seamen were sunk by diverse means,
In wartime by a bomber or (more likely) submarines,
Perchance to reach a lifeboat amid the death and strife,
Hoping to be picked up, conserving precious life.

With a ship abandoned the owners stopped your pay;
In truth the only real chance was rescue right away.
Survivors of such numerous crews were cast adrift at sea,
Not knowing of the end result whenever that would be.

Mal de mer was commonplace, in the troughs and peaks –
Exposure and the trauma went on for days or weeks:
Misery intense with sunburn and the thirst,
Hypothermia, overcrowding, or weather at its worst.

No comfort on the wooden thwarts, feet were always wet,
Capsizing or plain madness an ever constant threat,
Saltwater boils so painful in unrelenting spray,
And the need for bailing, constant every day.

The usual fare was biscuits a bit too dry to munch,
Unless crushed up with tinned milk, pulping them for lunch.
Perhaps if they were lucky there was Bovril pemmican,
Or Horlicks formed in tablets issued to each man.

Still not enough for voyages with survival at the fore,
Firm energy required for handling of the oar,
The wooden boats unwieldy, difficult to sail,
And progress near essential for ending their travail.

Fantastic feats of seamanship and courage went unsung,
Even after wartime when victory bells were rung.
Providence would play her part in this longest war,
In a vast and angry ocean a long way from the shore.

LIBERATE THE FALKLANDS

"The time has come", the British said, "to back up our demand,
Travel to the Falkland Isles and then reclaim our land."
Maritime logistics and forces set in motion
Took the war 8,000 miles across the mighty ocean.

Invincible and *Hermes* were the aircraft carriers,
Protected by our warships – and a couple of dozen Harriers.
Troops were sent on *Canberra* and the *QE2*,
Fuel and stores on merchantmen where the duster flew.

Admiral Sandy Woodward and Sea Lord Henry Leach
Commanded this armada and landings on the beach.
Below the waves our submarines watching all the way,
Sinking one big cruiser, then kept the rest at bay.

The junta sent the Exocet and Super Étendard;
Skyhawks and the Daggers were held in high regard,
Battles that were fought where the Argies made a stand
Varied from the bombing to fighting hand to hand.

The army did the yomping when their transport sadly sunk,
When Cunard`s *Conveyor*, was hit and turned to junk.
Commandos and the Paras went the extra mile
Over barren countryside, steadfast all the while.

Avro Vulcan bombers served us very proud,
Winging back from Stanley after strafing through the cloud.
A record set in history for the longest bombing flight
Proved a masterpiece of flying, through the day and night.

Galtieri showed his arrogance and made a bad mistake,
Thinking that old England would its land forsake.
We lost a lot of brave men, some aeroplanes and ships;
Fully laden landing craft suffered dreadful hits.

But the air force and the navy, army and marine,
Carried out their duty to country and the Queen,
And the merchant navy, under our red duster,
Special – indispensable when armadas have to muster.

Again reluctant heroes when the nation needs to fight,
Our sturdy unsung mariners showed their worth all right;
So raise a glass to Stanley, where once a white rag flew,
And all the ships that sailed there with a hearty crew.

Vital Need for Merchant Ships *– Up to the surrender in mid-June, forty merchantmen totalling over 500,000 gross registered tonnage reached the South Atlantic. Without them, the war would not have been won as the Royal Fleet Auxiliary lacked the ships to transport the land forces and then support them and the warships 8,000 miles from home.*

LIVE PORTRAIT

I cannot draw or paint, am tone deaf and cannot sing,
Have no artistic taint nor the money it may bring.
My canvas is the deep sea, but a brush I never clutch,
For the ever changing colours are impossible to touch,

But I have seen the lacy foam on the back of giant seas,
Looked upon the flying fish scudding in the breeze.
My eyes have noted albatross and spouting of blue whale,
Have marvelled at the dolphins, and clippers under sail.

The icebergs in the Arctic, far from desert sand,
Shining in the midnight sun in Rory Bory Land,
Freezing times in southern climes under stars so bright,
And – oh, so rare – a giant ray loop the loop in flight.

I have heard a storm's shrill wind a-whistling in the rigging,
And a mighty hurricane with nature wildly singing,
Worked through many sunsets and dawns of pastel hues,
Watched the daggered lighting strike wherever it may choose.

I have viewed the skeletons of ships now long deceased,
High and dry upon the banks of treacherous hidden reefs,
Ogled at the shark's attack with nothing left but blood,
And a foreign delta overwhelmed by flood.

Inspired by scuba diving in underwater caves,
Swum along an ancient wreck below the ocean waves,
Weathered blinding sandstorms blowing off the shore,
Fought against the tidal range that surged the river bore.

I have dodged the waterspout to avoid its whirling ire,
And gazed upon a metal mast beset by Elmo's fire.
Recognised a mirage and seen the rig set square
Upon the *Flying Dutchman* in a ghostly glare.

Does an artist sit too long while I sail from shore to shore?
Is he held in throng while I move along and free to see much more?
So young lad, a masterpiece may sit upon a shelf;
Better far a live portrait – go see it for yourself.

LIMERICK

There was an old sailor from Weston
Who sailed round the coast with his vest on.
He ventured too far
And crossed over the bar –
His funeral's on Monday in Preston.

LONELY AT THE BAR

The day is long – I'll chance upon a mate to share my woes.
I choose an inn – a cheerful place where everybody goes.
A motley crew should gather here; they come from not so far,
But alas, this day it's lonely – lonely at the bar.

No one to share my views with, or pass the oldest joke,
Insults flying here and there across like-minded folk,
To bandy words while quaffing from the cider jar,
Where have all my muckers gone? It's lonely at the bar.

I drink alone and think a bit of where my pals can be –
None of them teetotal, for all have been to sea,
But never mind – the barmaid's here to rib this ancient tar –
Maybe it's not so lonely, a-waiting at the bar.

March 2012

From an idea by Len Dibb Western.

LUCKY JIM

Now, Lucky Jim went off to sea a year before the war.
He was the luckiest man I think I ever saw,
For he was shipwrecked several times and managed to survive;
Men foundered all about him, but he ended up alive.

Sailing on a tramp when torpedoed by the Hun,
He was forced into a lifeboat and fired on with a gun,
Drifted for a while but not so very long.
That plunge was the first, so he called it number **one**.

Next, a loaded freighter exploded by a bomb –
He made it to a life raft and found the ship had gone.
He's not sure how he reached it – doesn't have a clue –
But eventually was rescued. That was number **two**.

Then he joined a coaster that hit a floating mine,
Dumped in freezing water and just picked up in time
By a passing trawler that hauled him from the sea.
A bit of hypothermia – and that was number **three**.

Another U-boat sunk him off the coast of Spain –
Steaming in a convoy, our Jim was saved again.
Jumping off a liner, sent to the ocean floor,
Then bending on to flotsam – that must be number **four**.

The next ship was a tanker that went up in a blaze.
This time he found a raft and clung there in a daze.
Under burning oil he'd had to duck and dive,
Losing many shipmates. Now this was number **five**.

He abandoned one of Hogarth's as it sunk beneath the waves.
Hurt and very hungry, he fought a gale for days.
Yet again was rescued, though in a pretty fix,
But Lucky Jim recovered – and that was number **six**.

When the war was over and things were not so grim
He told me of the sinkings and where he had to swim.
When asked his favourite digit, his eyes rolled up to heaven.
*"I'm not entirely sure, young man – but I hope it's number **seven**."*

LUCK

West of the Scottish Orkneys in October '39
A flotilla of our battleships steamed along in line,
The navy's grey destroyers patrolling on the flanks,
When a U-boat prowler found itself among the ranks.

It was unbelievable – a chance was heaven-sent –
A great attack position found without intent.
Right ahead was *Rodney*, then the *Nelson* and the *Hood*;
A full supply of tin fish – but none were any good.

From the German submarine, torpedoes hit their mark;
Incredibly those duds never caused a spark.
In disgust the Captain – Lieutenant William Zahn –
Lowered down his periscope then submerged and ran.

It was a great embarrassment to the Dönitz Kriegsmarine –
Aboard the flagship *Rodney* were VIPs supreme:
Sir Dudley Pound and Churchill with other admiral guys
Engaged on board for parley after *Royal Oak*'s demise.

I would call it fortunate at that time of the war
When underwater weapons sometimes failed to score.
There was no doubt about it – a dangerous place to be,
So lucky for the top brass and First Lord of the Sea!

*There were thirty-one U-boat attacks from favourable positions;
four attacks on the* Warspite, *twelve attacks on various cruisers,
ten attacks on destroyers and five attacks on troop transports. All
torpedoes failed to explode.*

MAL DE MER

Mal de mer they call it (seasick to you and me);
Many times I've seen it in my career at sea.
It's quite debilitating as you watch the colours rise –
Victims of this ailment stare from bloodshot eyes.

There's many names for spewing: a technicolor yawn,
Or on your knees in toilets, blowing down the horn.
They haven't found the sea legs to stand the corkscrew motion,
And wishing they were somewhere else instead of on the ocean.

The retching's pretty awful as the vessel leaps and races;
Pomposity is left behind as one loses airs and graces.
Just mention greasy bacon with eggs all soft and runny,
And suspect a lack of humour – they don't think it's funny.

Hanging on like grim death while heaving overside,
Contending with the nausea from Neptune's rolling ride,
They turn a deathly green – sometimes a pallid grey.
It's wise to stand to windward, keeping out the way.

If falling for this malady and feeling rather ill,
Perhaps a little queasy with no help from a pill,
Worry not, you'll cheer up when arriving in a lee –
The remedy for mal de mer is sit beneath a tree!

MERCHANT NAVY DAY

I see the ensigns flying; my heart fills with pride.
I see our colours carried, with seamen by my side.
I remember ships and mariners (and the debt we owe)
Now resting in the oceans, fathoms-deep below.

MERCHANT NAVY STAMP OF APPROVAL

Defeat was mighty close in the second greatest war –
Five thousand ships with cargoes sent to the ocean floor.
Merchant men were slaughtered sustaining our lifeline;
The country issued ration books, so desperate was the time.

A crisis on the home front – foodstuff very short,
Rations and provisions scarcely making port.
Convoys steaming steadfast under red ensigns
Faced demise from U-boats, the bombers and the mines.

There were many heroes on land and sea and air,
And 30,000 seamen gave their lives out there,
Transporting reinforcements, resources and supplies,
And fuel to fly the Spitfires fighting in the skies.

Perhaps we should commend them by illustrating stamps
With the freighters and the liners, the tankers and the tramps.
It would be a special tribute, rather overdue,
To mariners who manned them and a way to say thank you.

MY SON

"Now young lad, please tell me and drink this cup of tea:
Why are you so down and sad when you come home from sea?"

"It's just the seaman's life, Mother, and sailing on a scow,
Plus leaving all my family, that bothers me right now."

"No, there's something in your eyes, young man, I've never seen before.
They seem to stare like I'm not there. Please tell me, I implore."

"It's just the brutal war, Mother, when I steam across the foam,
Perchance to meet the enemy – a sitting duck alone."

"There's something in your heart, young man. I hear you wake at night.
In your dream I think you've seen much more to give you fright."

"It's just the sight beheld, Mother, at the slaughter of my mates,
Their ship disintegrated – torpedoed in the Straits."

"There's something in your face, my boy, that tells me what you know.
Stay at home, refuse to roam, remain with me – don't go."

"Mother dear, be brave. I cannot stay with you –
Even though a civvy, I have a job to do.
My place to be is the cruel sea, riding on the swell
With men like me – don't you see? – until we're sent to hell."

"What will be the point, young man. What's the use, I say,
To risk your life in voyage strife to earn so little pay?"

"Oh, Mother dear, 'tis quite clear it's not for wage reward.
You can be sure I'm a seaman pure, so I will sail abroad,
For they need our merchant navy to save our precious land.
Day and night we board our ships – without a farewell band."

"So that's what it's all about, my son – our freedom to defend.
On unyielding mariners I know we can depend."

"Sorry, Mum – when beaten low and spirits start to sag,
Duty calls for country beneath our merchant flag.
These are desperate cargoes that really must get through –
The time is near, I'll pack my gear and join another crew."

"Bless you, son. I understood when you took your ship to sea,
You sailed and died, but went with pride to go down in history.
Old shipmates built your monument on a quay down Bristol way –
It's where I weep and talk to you, recalling our last day."

MOLLY MOGGS' DRAG SHOW

It's the greatest show for sailors when they roll in from sea,
With trannies and the queens imparting repartee,
Singing songs from music halls down old memory lanes,
Playing with their posies or forming daisy chains.

They stick up for each other and over backwards bend –
The proof is in the pudding with the ackers that they send.
So here's to Molly Moggs' and all gender types within,
For raising funds for heroes with donations in a tin.

MY HEROES

Speak not to me of heroes unless they served at sea.
Men that have the Nelson touch – they're the ones for me.
They sailed the coast of England and all the globe around,
Saviours of our country that our blue lanes surround.

Whether past or future – admiral or not –
Takes a special breed of man to take a sailor's lot,
From wooden ships and iron men sent out to explore,
To keeping lifelines flowing in desperate times of war.

Oiling wheels of commerce, fighting all the way,
Engaging with the enemy, the weather every day,
Steaming in the convoys, risking life and limb,
Or sailing bowsprit-under at a typhoon's whim.

The hardy Western Ocean men you cannot disregard,
Or those that manned the tea clippers, reefing on the yard,
Maybe in a submarine in claustrophobic space,
Perhaps upon an oil rig in a godforsaken place.

The pilots and the tug men that work the clock around,
At the end of voyages docking safe and sound,
Lifeboat crews and fishermen – all that do their share!
So take me back to sea, boys – my heroes are all there.

NEW COLOURS

Wijsmuller's bought the Cory tugs – we painted them anew.
Out went the red from funnels – now they're black and blue.
The buff was covered over, first with undercoat,
White gloss then applied to the housing round the boat.

On the monkey island, the fishplate and surround,
Lucent Day-Glo orange may be seen for miles around.
The mast also painted blue by dangling from a chair,
Contending with the banjo bits while hanging in the air.

The hull was swapped to blue where it butts against the tide,
With grey upon the decks and bulwarks at the side.
The windlass and the towing winch were changed from ancient green,
Standing out so proudly with their new-found sheen.

All the tugs in Avonmouth were quite an apparition –
The colours of the rainbow while going through transition.
Now steaming down the channel they look a handsome sight,
With all the brand-new paintwork shining nice and bright.

It hasn't changed old Cory's men although we wear fresh coat;
These hardy crews are much the same on all our tugs afloat.
I suppose we'll have an issue of a dictionary in Dutch,
But we refuse to wear the clogs – that's a little bit too much!

NO KHAZI ON THE COACH!

We took a trip to Weymouth seventy miles away,
To march along and celebrate the annual Veterans Day.
Our be-medalled passengers and ladies didn't fuss:
No stopping on the way, boys – sans toilet on the bus.

A lengthy time to celebrate and sample of the grog,
A mug of tea partaken – perhaps the hair of dog.
Water, water everywhere until the sun came out,
Then a pint of ale or two squirted from the spout.

You may be understanding the essence of my drift
If I mention ancient bladders and p---pots for a gift,
Steaming home non-stop, cross-legged on approach.
"What," you say, amazed, *"no khazi on the coach!"*

'Bristol MNA trip to Weymouth and back,
24 June 2012.

NEXT?

As I was resting on my bunk
Thoughts of last night – ships were sunk –
Were of this convoy steaming east
And a wolf pack's frenzied feast.

Our ship I ponder – my turn next?
Cannot slumber – mind so vexed.
Ten more days will see us through,
But will the U-boats strike anew?

Orphaned children, wives bereft,
As vessels founder – flotsam left.
Will I greet my shipmates safe ashore,
Or be lost for evermore?

Just any time it seems to be
Torpedoes dart across the sea.
Will they strike the engine room
Or in the hold with massive boom?

Whether killed in one fell swoop
Or linger dying on the poop,
I'm thinking of my dear old mum,
Grieving for her youngest son.

Would I be blasted from the deck
To blazing water round my neck?
Perhaps I'll make it to a boat,
Or – if I'm injured – will I float?

Mind in turmoil and raw emotion,
Must I die in the mighty ocean?
So many ships, so many crew
Perished here – survivors few.

But if we make it safe and sound,
We'll sail again, outward-bound.
What hope now of peaceful sleep
While gently rolling 'cross the deep?

NO MORE FEAR OF U-BOATS

It was fine to sail away again when the war was ended,
Free to show the steaming lights as the law intended.
No more expecting tin fish to explode at any time,
Or convoy station keeping, maintaining of the line.

Deadlights could be opened so air could circulate,
A smoke on deck permissible if sanctioned by the mate,
Lifeboats in their davits now snugly stowed inboard,
And using chipping hammers on the way abroad.

No more fear of U-boats and their wicked games,
But plenty floating mines about, broken free of chains.
Flashing via an Aldis lamp with his fingertips,
The mate could chat in Morse code openly to ships.

Wartime grey was changed to colours with some cheer
(They took the puny guns off, but left degaussing gear),
So all was back to normal, just fighting lousy weather,
And engines up to full speed going hell for leather.

It's fine to strike the bells again, marking off the time,
Not forgetting shipmates that left us in their prime.
Most are under deep sea, in a sunken tomb,
As we sail into sunshine – after years of gloom.

ODE TO A MOTHER-IN-LAW

A face with a thousand wrinkles – she'd come to do her hair.
In the kitchen near the pickles she was sitting there
Wearing an old red towel, her tresses not so fine.
The wife stuck all the rollers in, resembling porcupine.
She added then the chemicals – the smell was quite atrocious,
Sending out an awful stink, a bit like halitosis.
Next she put the dryer on – won't hear what I say.
I cannot make the coffee – guess who's in the way?
Checking in the mirror, looking for the roots,
All her bracelets jangling – the ones she bought in Boots,
Gossiping with slander and slurping mugs of tea,
Wolfing down the biscuits like a refugee.
Spouting off on politics and stinking of Old Spice,
Her diet's shot out the window, but she's giving me advice.
Then came the tearful bit amongst the diatribe:
The picture of adversity because her cat had died.
Continuing the treatment and all that it entails,
Gets the scarlet varnish out to paint her fingernails.
Soon she's gazing happy with the powder and the paint,
Gathering up her normal face – of a persecuted saint.
She ups and lights a ciggy – doesn't really care,
Leaving piles of fag ash underneath the chair.
Thinks she's looking sexy, gives me a dirty leer,
Then she goes and helps herself – to my favourite beer.
She tells me that the daughters turn out just like mothers,
Reminding me quite starkly while hitching up her udders.
Now she feels quite beautiful, she smiles and looks at me;
I have a sudden feeling I should be miles away at sea.

OLD SAILORS

Old sailors like to drink a bit and talk of days of yore,
To greet the hands that sailed the ships that now have gone before.
These lads have seen the best of men, and oftentimes the worst,
But now they love a drink or two to quench their salty thirst.

Recalling nights in foreign bars when they stood upon the table
To sing the songs of sailor men that were heard for 'most a cable,
Reciting verse like 'Dead-Eye Dick', 'Magrew' and 'Eskimo Nell',
The rousing words of ballads and of Kipling they would tell.

It's swell to go out with your mates again to have a drop of cheer,
To recall the days of a dinner-time session when still in your working gear.
Yes, it's good to meet another crew, and those from a previous ship,
To have a yarn and a laugh once more, a tot and a merry quip.

A storm, a fire or injury – whatever lay in store –
Was covered by resourcefulness you'd never see ashore.
These are the times they talk about, and recall with honest pleasure.
"Come on, Bos', another one – here's a double measure."

They rode the mighty oceans when the seas were rolling white,
And they saw the hungry days when the land was out of sight.
Then came wandering home again, no matter where they'd been,
Sighting whales and flying fish where the blue sea turns to green.

So it's wonderful to chew the fat, right up to seven bells,
To argue with your shellback friends till the landlord loudly yells.
They remember ports in distant lands – the ones well known to sailors –
And the hand-stitched suits they swaggered in, made by the Chinese tailors.

It matters not what rank you were when the barman takes your money,
Or how they spin the hyperbole to make the facts so funny.
It does 'em good to swing the lamp and talk of many things,
For they will chat to anyone from lonely tramps to kings.

The wife she says you're 'crackers' to go sinking pints once more,
But in her heart she knows – when you roll through the door –
That you've sailed the Western Ocean, and your time was not in vain,
Cos those old men were shipmates – brought back to life again.

OH, TO SAIL ON TUGS AGAIN!

Oh, to sail on the tugs again in the bustling Avon docks,
To tow ships in and out again through Royal Portbury Locks,
On the *Westgarth* and the *Portgarth* or the *Gilbert* under the bow,
Or perhaps the *Avongarth* – I think of her just now!

Oh, to steam down the channel again in the fierceness of the tide,
Ready, eager and willing with a good mate by my side,
Then go home in the morning, after docking one in the murk,
Bucking lines of traffic when everyone's going to work!

Oh, to be at the wheel again while towing round the pier,
Our hawser tight and stretching as the knuckle comes steadily near,
With skill of the crew that man them, the best and salt of the earth,
And the "Job well done" from the pilots when safely in their berth!

Oh, to attend in the summer when the weather can be nice,
But not so great in the winter with treacherous fog and the ice!
Hauling various craft about with freight of every type,
The picnic element's missing when working there all night.

Oh, to complete a job again after gales and worry,
Then return to 'tie up' and scamper home in a hurry!
For soon we'll have new orders from the next tide's busy sheet,
Followed by some maintenance all throughout the fleet.

Oh, to hear the engines from the quietness of my home
As the tugs put on the power and haul one over the foam!
Then it goes to remind me of arduous hours that are long.
Happily I creep back to bed – my tug-boat days are gone.

OLD VETERANS

In bloom of life they sailed away,
At sea along with peers.
They kept the lifelines flowing
Amid the U-boat fears.

There they lost their shipmates
That never did grow old,
Though veterans remember
As advancing years unfold.

They saw the perils of the deep,
The best and worst in men,
Grieving with compatriots
In the war back then.

Now these reluctant heroes,
For them no grave, the deep –
Progressively they cross the bar,
A rendezvous to keep.

ON POPPY DAY

On Poppy Day I march again,
In wind or shine, sometimes rain,
For those who went and fought in wars,
Then gave their lives for some just cause.

Perhaps they fell in foreign lands,
Or lost at sea with all hands.
Each one answered freedom's call.
Remember them – God bless 'em all.

In silence then I blink my tears,
Side by side with medalled peers,
A surge of tribute uppermost
At the sounding of last post.

On Poppy Day we march again,
Stepping out to band's refrain,
Veterans' bearing justly proud,
Passing by the loyal crowd.

OUR ADMIRALS

Let's drink to British admirals, from Nelson to Lord West,
For presiding over mariners who deserve the best,
On naval ships from anywhere that sail out on the tide,
Now including submarines stemming from the Clyde.

They know our merchant ships, under our red duster,
Are paramount importance in convoys when they muster.
Protection and our freedom is always what we need –
It's the navy that defends them with men of special breed.

Always in the background, or maybe at the fore,
There's an admiral accountable in peace or ghastly war.
They deal with politicians and take a bit of heat,
Liable for actions all throughout the fleet.

From recruitment to the building of modern fighting craft,
To gunnery and weapons bristling fore and aft,
They use their great authority linked with expertise
For maintenance and vigilance on the seven seas.

You know our island history: we never will be slaves –
Not as long as admirals help us rule the waves.

OUTWARD-BOUND

I remember well when I went off to sea
Many years ago, but things come back to me:
Sights and sounds of seamen on a merchant ship,
Just the same around the world, however long the trip.

Familiar life of ship's routine as she steams from A to B,
A following wind and gentle swell as the vessel's running free,
Seagulls over the quarter awaiting galley gash,
Wingtips hardly moving till they see their breakfast splash.

A roving British tanker passing close to port,
Flying from her gaff red duster whipping taut,
The flying fish and porpoise playing round the bow –
All these things and many more I recall just now.

Lookout on the fo'c'sle with sound of the bow wave's swish,
Or on the monkey island with the foghorn's constant hiss,
Perhaps upon the masthead, high up in the air,
Dangling from its lizard a waiting bosun's chair.

Work is done upon the charts as the mates plot out our course;
Aft the bridge in his radio shack Sparkie taps his Morse;
Engineer in overalls walking round with spanner,
And constant turning on the spot – the modern radar scanner.

A handy crowd out on deck equipped with knife and spike,
The steady wake when looking aft – all due to Iron Mike.
Buffer in his locker – a thimble in the vice –
Showing young apprentices the Ozzy locking splice.

The general work and maintenance of topping lifts and guys,
The pulsing of the engine (not noticed till it dies);
Chippy with his sounding rod, plumbing all the tanks;
A growing tan while heading south and beards among the ranks.

Greasers wearing sweat rags, and buckles back to front,
Telling yarns of wartime days and calling cook a runt.
We rarely see the master until it's Sunday rounds;
His authority is silent unless there are the grounds.

But most of all we're ready for hazards on the way –
Peril, fog or tempest will surely come one day.
I learned the ways of mariners with an independent crew.
How I loved those salad days! I 'spect that you did too.

OUR VETERANS

Once on the quay at Welsh Back I saw our veterans stand –
Time and care had reached them, over sea and land.

But now you'll see in passing, on seats erected here,
The nameplates of our heroes, in memory held dear.

They chanced their lives for country, asked not the reason why,
The Nelson touch abiding within a sparking eye.

The long todays of youth soon pass, in this living game;
Tomorrows seemed so far away – they risked them just the same.

By sailing in our convoys across the devil seas,
Still our duster flutters because of men like these.

OVER THE SEA AND FAR AWAY
(To the tune of 'Over the Hills and Far Away')

Convoys formed – brave men aboard, battened down to go abroad,
Sailing out from friendly bay, over the sea and far away.
Perils faced from bomber's run, torpedoes, mines or raider's gun,
Seamen braced for come what may, over the sea and far away.

Keeping lifelines going strong through a voyage fraught and long,
Storms and fog and icy spray, over the sea and far away.
Vital cargoes must get through, past a wolf pack's hostile view,
Under threatening clouds of grey, over the sea and far away.

Freighters ventured young and old – many die in ocean cold.
Liners, tankers – all were prey, over the sea and far away.
Day and night every crew feared a bombshell from the blue;
Still they went to earn their pay, over the sea and far away.

Violent times whereupon steadfast men and ships rolled on.
Duty called and had its say, over the sea and far away.
Remember well a seaman's war lest we forget on freedom's shore
Their red ensign flies today, over the sea and far away.

PQ 17

A convoy bound for Russia in July of '42
Gathered off old Reykjavik in Iceland's summer hue.
Thirty-five big freighters laden with supplies
Sailing in the midnight sun – some thought it was unwise.

Still a perilous journey, rolling like a log,
With the sea spray freezing and banks of icy fog,
Across the Arctic Ocean, all without a lee,
Toward the north of Norway to the Barents Sea.

Steaming ever watchful, ticking off the hours,
Shepherded by navy ships with their fighting powers,
Including three destroyers, guarding, yet again,
Stores to move an army of 50,000 men.

Back at home in London the Admiral Dudley Pound
Sent a message to his navy: 'You will withdraw westbound.'
The cause of this dire action to the Admiral was plain:
The Germans sailed their surface ships and Tirpitz was to blame.

The stunned escort commander his orders must obey –
Turned his men at full speed and sent them all away.
From his cruisers to the convoy the signal lamp did chatter:
"Sorry, lads, to leave you, but convoy now must scatter."

Though Tirpitz left her moorings there wasn't any threat;
Unhappily, the powers that be didn't know that yet.
Thus we had the convoy dispersed and all spread out,
At the mercy of the Luftwaffe and U-boats thereabout.

Now the deadly onslaught on July the 4th began –
The sinking of the *Carlton, William Hooper, Zaafaran,
Paulus Potter, River Afton, Navarino, Honomu,*
The *Pancraft* and the *Earlston, Dan Morgan* just a few.

Many ships were doomed – they numbered twenty-four
With their vital cargoes sent to the ocean floor.
Misleading information meant brave men went to die,
Left without protection, knew not the reason why.

*Just part of the cargoes lost on the PQ17 included 3,350 motor
vehicles, 430 tanks, 210 bombers, radar sets and ammunition. The
exact number of men lost is not known.*

PROGRESS

Master and commander standing there at ease
Braced upon his quarterdeck eyeing up the breeze,
Mainsail tight, ballooning, disciplined and squared,
Sheets hauled aft and ready, belaying pins prepared,
Men upon the futtock shrouds scrambling to the yard,
Braces taut and straining, bowing very hard.

Captain in his swivel chair, radar by his side,
Pushing coloured buttons to manoeuvre in the tide,
Thrusters pushing easily, taking it in turn,
Automatic sensors at the bow and stern,
Seamen wearing plastic hats and overalls that glow,
Pulling little levers that make the winches go.

Progress!

RAY PEARCE, MN, 1925–2004

He never mentioned it before, not until this year.
Never wanted to – it disturbed and sprang a tear.
Torpedoed there in one ship – he had not told a soul
When recalling his old shipmates in a dreadful waiting role.

For he was in a lifeboat with sixteen other men –
A few of them were injured – could do nought for them.
One of them was badly burnt, within his roasted skin,
Memory so traumatic – he'd felt so much for him.

He told a bit to you guys – now the time has gone.
These men died in agony, departing one by one.
Two days in a lifeboat – death reigned there supreme.
Ray he was not injured, but a lad of mere sixteen.

There were many unsung heroes in the war at sea;
This is one example, for it seems to me
They carried out their duties, neither bragged nor spoke:
Seafarers with the Nelson touch – and mighty hearts of oak.

February 2004

From an interview in 2003 with Ray and Age Exchange of London.

RAYMOND VICTOR STEED

A galley boy named Raymond Steed joined the *Empire Morn*
At the docks in Newport, close where he was born.
In the merchant navy now, but only just fourteen,
He'd gone to sail in convoys – fighting-fit and keen.

Nineteen forty-three it was; aggression in full flow,
Unmindful of the danger, he couldn't wait to go.
Ray carried out his duties, earning meagre pay,
Until alas, in April, his world was blown away.

Not far off Casablanca, the *Empire* struck a mine
Laid there by a U-boat with purpose and design.
The consequent explosion set cargo blasting then,
Killing brave young Raymond and twenty other men.

His body's in Morocco, near the road to Marrakesh,
In a nurtured cemetery, surroundings trim and fresh.
He was the youngest seaman to go and lose his life
While standing firm in jeopardy mid the wartime strife.

Greater than 500 boys were sent to Neptune's floor –
Sixteenth birthdays never met, lost for evermore.
They helped sustain our lifelines in a hostile time at sea,
Those young and unsung heroes that sailed for you and me.

RELUCTANT HEROES

This island race has many sons who natural went to sea –
Salt water in their veins stemmed from our history.
They did not sail to fight a war or oppose the mighty Hun;
These merchant men were hardy souls – they did not want a gun.

But when the conflict started and the nation called to fight,
The mariners of Britain were targets day and night.
From galley boy to master, of the liner and the tramp,
From engineer to bosun – all men that swung the lamp.

Even though civilians, from the shires and from the town,
They turned and did their duty to the public and the crown.
Torpedoed, bombed and shot at, they carried on their trade,
The lifeline of the country – with a seagull serenade.

They brought fuel and ammunition so the aircraft could defend;
Food and goods were ferried until the bitter end.
The price to pay was heavy to haul those precious tons,
With only guts to fight with – of our seafaring sons.

Life at sea is fraught enough with peril every quarter,
But try a bomb right through the plates and crushing tons of water.
This may come at any time while toiling or repose,
With little chance and many dead – we will remember those.

For six long years they persevered and hardly went ashore;
Everything was given – you could not ask for more.
They did not seek publicity or actively dissent,
Just climbed aboard and steamed away wherever they were sent.

When the war was over, the foe called it a day;
Our mariners shipped out again – in their peaceful way.
Now when you see a monument to our fighting kin,
Salute our merchant navy – and our valiant crews within.

RIO DE JANEIRO

My mouth is as dry as a biscuit, my head a throbbing drum –
We'd been ashore in Rio and sampled local rum.
We were the crew of the *Roscoe* – one of Lamport and Holt's.
The booze was red and rusty with a kick of a thousand volts.

In the tropical evening we had started our foray,
Attracted to a nightclub on this a Saturday;
We'd wandered out for a quiet night and a twirl around the floor
With the ladies employed there and some that came in the door.

Quite happy we were while dancing and having a bit of a smooch,
Spending our hard-earned money on girls and dynamite hooch.
All smart we were in our tee shirts and freshly washed blue jeans,
When all of a sudden they entered – the United States Marines.

You've heard about the red rag and what it did to the bull –
It seemed we weren't so welcome, although the place was full.
We tolerant British sailors – well, we never turned a hair,
But it seems the Yankee 'crew cuts' did not like us there.

It may have been just jealousy or dancing with their dames,
But when they'd had a drink or two they began to call us names.
We had to stand our corner – we thought it only right
To honour merchant seamen and stand up for a fight.

So with this altercation we had a bit of fun –
Everything went flying, including lots of rum,
Chairs and tables over and a window there stove in,
Fists and knuckles bruising, connecting with a chin.

Everyone enjoyed it – we had the upper hand.
Even the marines did, and most of them were canned;
But someone called the MPs – they came roaring up in Jeeps.
They weren't entirely partial, so we ducked into the streets.

In a bar of safety we counted up the cost:
A couple of broken nosebleeds an' a tin of baccy lost.
So *Roscoe*-bound we made it, knowing valour prevailed;
We turned to prompt next morning, and later on we sailed.

The Captain's log was open as he sat there with a grin,
Scribing down the truth, of course – official now therein.
Before the book snapped shut I saw he'd written down:
'All the crew ashore last night – a quiet night on the town!'

ROYAL NAVY-SPEAK

There's a lot of things that seamen say that seem to give 'em pleasure.
They see the world and all about – and that's not always leisure.
But the navy has a language – they made it 'most their own;
You'll not always hear it though, unless Jack's on leave at home.

To ring eight bells is crossed the bar or dead to shoreside men,
An' if you heard of Jack with bumps, of course, well, that's a Wren.
Jack Dusty and Jam Bosun, they are masters of the store.
Jews march past is check your purse after a night ashore.

They also speak of choppers – the ones that sort of fly –
Known as angry palm trees that go for a flutter by.
The Jesus nut is the main one that holds the rotor on,
And gattling gobs are talkers who chat too much or long.

Underpants are rompers, where the knicker python's stowed,
Ready to use a playpen where'er his girlfriend's towed.
And the morning sickness, with the ladies' dodgy tummy,
Then it's called Egyptian flu cos she's going to be a mummy.

Bombay runners are roaches that run around and sting.
Turd tank for the rectum, and wire is electric string.
Night fighters are the coloured chaps; neck oil is suds or beer.
Sparrow fart is the break of day, and hat rack is the queer.

Hitler's victuallers, the catering staff that bring the men some grub.
The pond is the Atlantic, raise the peepstick on a sub.
Humungus is enormous – that you ought to know.
An Arctic fox is a frozen turd lying in the snow.

Stagger juice is rum, and squitters are the trots.
Porridge guns are bagpipes played by the friendly Scots.
A swindle sheet, an expenses claim or similar type of caper.
The circular file, a basket – one for chucking paper.

A great big pavement pizza, when someone's been a little sick.
And siphoning the python, when you fancy pumping ship.
It's the devil-dodging padre that's called the amen wallah,
Also named the sin bosun and noted by his collar.

Plus the Irish hurricane – a flat calm, I suppose.
Irish mail is a bag of spuds, and snot box is the nose.
Henpecked is a hangover from drinking Famous Grouse.
Goodbye now from the hermit box – the Captain's little house.

RETURN TO MALTA

This creed of men, this breed of men that came back from the war,
These merchant men, these doughty men, returned to Malta's shore,
These British men from motley crews – for men that didn't come back –
Were there to join the residents at the laying of a plaque.

These old lads caused mayhem from the moment they touched down,
But hearts were in the right place at Valletta's ancient town.
These veterans, with their standards, mustered at St Paul's,
Unveiled our marble tribute between the trumpet calls.

Recalling all those shipmates that never did grow old,
I saw the backbones stiffen as emotions took a hold.
They remembered 'Pedestal' and other convoys there –
It seemed that nature joined us with thunder in the air.

Gale-force winds were blowing and hailstones from the sky
While listening to the sermon that made a hard man cry.
Attending then the palace, 'longside the Bishop's throne,
The President, de Marco, told of his siege at home.

Among the various stories that VIPs narrated
Was a tale of two young sisters that were promptly educated
By the saying of the grace – prior to the daily meal –
Learning that the food they ate sprung from men's ordeal.

This yarn is true I relay to you – from letters signed by name.
Old ladies now, but grateful still, they wore the 'hood of shame'.
They wrote of when their father – before he poured the gravy –
Prayed:

"For what we are about to receive, may the Lord make us truly thankful –
And for the merchant navy."

SAIL ON

Sail on, my friends, in convoy's keep;
Leave me here in the deep to sleep.
I watch you go midst bubbling wake;
You will not stop – too much at stake.

Sail on, old friends. My ship's gone down –
It won't be long before I drown.
Tell my loved ones – all that knew me –
"Torpedo's target – lost at sea."

Sail on, my friends. You may survive;
Our vital cargoes must arrive.
Take a drink if you reach port;
Remember me – give me a thought.

Steam on, young seamen – go full speed.
Our country's at it's greatest need.
I give my life for other's bread.
Farewell, mates – now I'm dead.

ROLLING HOME IN CONVOYS, 1939–45

Rolling home in convoys five miles wide or more,
Our hardy merchant seamen await the night in store.
A crawling speed of eight knots from Halifax to home,
Escorts interweaving, darting though the foam.

The wolf pack will be lurking, waiting in advance,
To shoot a damn torpedo when they have a chance.
These men that run the gauntlet are wary all the time,
Hoping that their own ships avoid the firing line.

Keen to get the cargo through, but sitting like a duck,
Trusting to the navy boys and large amounts of luck,
Fearing of forsaken ships and fires that light the sky,
Foretelling of the danger as fine men sink and die.

Countermeasures not so good against the U-boats' tricks,
Resulting in foul carnage and spreading oily slicks;
Staunchly sailing on through the weeks of dread,
Keeping lifelines open while flying flags of red.

Some steaming back to Liverpool and also to the Clyde,
Freighters bound for Barry and Avonmouth's big tide.
Tankers make for jetties all around our shores,
With extra miles zigzagging, making wide detours.

Still they run the risk of colliding with a mine,
Or bombing from a Kondor patrolling over brine,
Plus the usual hazards known to all seadogs:
Hurricanes and storms or blinding ghostly fogs.

When and if they sail through, after trips of trial,
Seamen don a brave face with grim or cheery smile.
They'll endure the war till victory bells are rung,
Then carry on seafaring – bravery unsung.

SAMUEL PLIMSOLL

Good old Samuel Plimsoll – he was the seaman's friend.
He stood against shipowners in order to defend
Basic rights and safety on all seagoing trips,
By bringing legislation to deadly 'coffin-ships'.

A Liberal politician – a caring man for sure –
Born near docks in Redcliffe in 1824.
Long and hard in Parliament he fought to have a say;
Eventually this Bristol man won and had his way.

Excessive was the loss of life and so much common slaughter,
By sailing on decrepit craft too low in the water,
For many vessels left the quay, soon to sink right under,
Though well insured the cargoes of ships that broke asunder.

Men were thought expendable for the sake of profit;
Wicked were the shipowners who made their money off it.
Countless crews protested, all to no avail,
Refusing work on rotten ships – ending up in jail.

Many rights for mariners were plenty overdue.
Samuel saw at first-hand, so knew just what do:
He wrote about our seamen and perils shore to shore,
Urging for improvements and making them the law.

Soon the Merchant Shipping Act of 1876
Demanded annual surveys, so measured marks affixed
Upon the hull of all ships to denote a legal draught,
Assisting in the buoyancy measured fore and aft.

There is a bust of Plimsoll here in Bristol city –
A reminder yet of seamen, of those he took such pity,
And homage to a great man in memory of those days
When life was even harder upon our blue seaways.

SEA CADETS

('Ready, aye, ready')

This island place will always be a natural seaman's home,
While protecting or transporting cargoes o'er the foam.
The finest seamen in the world with training in their youth
Must still uphold our heritage by skill and basic truth.

A good start is the Sea Cadets, if twelve years old and keen
To open up one's options while working in a team.
Boys and girls are taught in most things maritime,
Practical and theory, by instructors in their prime.

What better for a youngster than marching to the band,
Or climbing up the rigging, reaching high by hand!
Restricted not by race or creed, but challenges anew,
Nor politics or militants to steer another's view.

Based upon traditions of naval origin,
Well founded are the virtues of discipline within.
They have the tall ship *Royalist* to hone their latent skills,
But now require a new brig to learn from thrills and spills.

The need is quite imperative for a training craft,
For continuing instruction on a vessel fore and aft.
With training and encouragement the will is in their clutch –
Perhaps the birth of leadership and the Nelson touch.

We should aid our Sea Cadets and help them all to grow,
Feed them great potential – extend the status quo,
For Britain's breed of mariners are the very best,
Stemming from our youngsters expressing interest.

I was a member of Reading Sea Cadet Corps, Jervis Bay, from 1953 to 1956.

MERCHANT NAVY DAY, 3 SEPTEMBER (1)

Take a little care this day and glance above the tiles,
Perchance to see a flagpole visible for miles,
Atop of it a red flag proudly whipping tight,
A merchant-navy ensign flying there by right.

From important buildings as well as from the sea,
It's flown to honour mariners and shipping history
Sailing through the years, transporting all the freight,
Conserving of the lifelines, keeping Britain great.

If you glance aloft and see with knowing eye
A duster at the masthead when you're passing by,
Please inform your offspring while going on to say,
"A debt is owed to seamen under colours flown today."

MERCHANT NAVY DAY, 3 SEPTEMBER (2)

I see the ensigns flying, my heart fills with pride.
I see our colours carried with seamen by my side.
I remember ships and mariners (and the debt we owe)
Now resting in the oceans, fathoms deep below.

MERCHANT NAVY DAY, 3 SEPTEMBER (3)

Our country celebrates centenaries and the Cenotaph's just cause.
We remember airmen and soldiers from the wars,
The navy and civilians and miners from the pit,
Royalty and land girls – all those that did their bit.

Now the merchant navy has its special say,
Flying its red ensign on the third September day
From our public buildings in Britain and abroad,
So the population may look up and applaud.

Reminding everybody of the sacrifice they made,
Shipping vital cargoes in a mortal wartime trade,
Mostly sailing unarmed or with very poor defence,
Casualties and losses were appalling and immense.

Round the world they voyaged 'cross oceans near and far,
Magnetic mines abundant on both sides of the bar,
Torpedoes launched from U-boats, bombs aimed from the sky,
Salvoes fired from raiders, intent that ships would die.

Often in awful conditions, at work in numbing cold,
Through voracious seas of the Arctic with explosives in the hold,
Or the white heat of the tropics, steaming into hell,
Living on tons of petrol, dreading the enemy's shell.

Our lads ran the gauntlet, braving marauder's might,
Showing a stubborn red duster every day of the fight.
If they survived, they returned – not once, but again and again.
Hence lifeblood brought to nations by indefatigable men.

On all the seas and rivers where British seamen go,
From the tropics to the edges of where the icebergs grow,
You will see the ruddy bunting of bright or smoky red –
It's our merchant-navy ensign flying overhead.

SHIP HIGH IN TRANSIT

Manure was carried by sea, my friend, many years ago,
Mostly dried and stowed in sacks in the hold below.
Oftentimes in those days the ships did spring a leak,
Wetting fertiliser and causing such a reek.

Then began a problem, for it turned to methane gas –
A single spark or candle flame, and up she went, alas!
Lessons then were learnt, so the stuff was stowed up high –
Crucial now, important, to keep the cargo dry.

Marked upon the manifest and on the bags were writ,
'Ship High In Transit' – true origin, my friend,
Of the word we know as ****.

SINGAPORE

Flying south to Sydney, I stopped at Singapore,
Under threat of punishment if I broke the law.
From the elegance of Raffles to the red-light part of town,
Everyone's obedient – no one lets you down.

The Tiger beer is legal and you may smoke outside,
But better not get drunk, my friend, or cast that fag aside.
The weather's always lovely beneath this equator sun,
But don't attempt the jaywalking for the jail is not much fun.

You dare not raise your voice or even point your finger,
Must not swear or argue else your feet will scarcely linger.
No talk of unemployment, no mention of a dole;
There is no begging on the street whatever state your soul.

There's plenty bits of greenery among the city sprawl,
Where the state-erected notices warning one and all
'Keep off the Grass', 'Don't Wait Here', 'No dogs allowed this side',
'No Rubbish Dumped' – quite obvious as I took a taxi ride.

Everything is clinical as delights I tried to savour
When touring round the town – on my best behaviour.
The people look so miserable – no one seems to laugh,
While avoiding all the litter bins that clutter up the path.

But I had this awful feeling that gave me quite a fright
That I would break a law somehow and miss my outward flight.
Then it slowly dawned on me – I'm not afraid of muggers,
I'm wary of the opposite, them crime-prevention buggers!

On my immigration card, boldly writ in red,
In no uncertain terms the statement starkly said,
'Death to all drug traffickers under Singaporee law.'
Well, I'd smuggled in some baccy and bottles – three or four.

The customs never found them cos I hid them out the way,
But happy then I guess I was – to fly out again next day.

February 2002

119

SMOKY JOE'S

Now, the British merchant seaman, he works so hard at sea.
In times of rest he likes a drink – well, that's OK with me.
I remember one occasion down at Smoky Joe's –
It's on the Bluff at Durban, as many a sailor knows.

Like the staithes at Dunston, there's miles of railroad track.
Beyond a coaling station stood a collier's drinking shack –
A wood shebeen with oil drums on a bed of cindered coke.
We savoured native brandy – it was known as old 'Cape smoke'.

I know we had a good day as we drank and swung the lamp.
Alas, our poor old bosun, he flaked out like a tramp.
My mate and I took charge of him, now he'd spent his bucks –
By one leg each we tugged him home, beneath the railroad trucks.

The Bosun now was sixty-eight, but still as hard as nails –
He never did complain as his head banged on the rails.
We did our best to get him back – I suppose we were his keepers.
He was mainly horizontal as he bumped along the sleepers.

Our next day's work was heavy after boozing at the bar:
Lifting down the hatch boards and coating them with tar.
The temperature was ninety, but the Buffer pressed his men.
(He went to sea in sailing ships at the age of ten.)

He toiled as hard as anyone and earned our great respect –
For all the contact with his skull he showed no ill effect,
Ignoring cuts and bruises and without a hint of pain.
Evening came – he had a shave then went ashore again.

We went and tapped the steward and drew another sub;
Once more we climbed the timbers to Smoky Joe's rough pub.
This time we hauled the old man back as careful as we could –
We dragged him by his arms, so his feet bounced on the wood!

SOMETIMES

Sometimes a ship's at anchor, riding in a lee.
Sometimes a ship's just steaming – clear and running free.
Sometimes a ship's in dry dock, a-mending of her plates.
Sometimes a ship's near hove to in a gale across the Straits.

Well, that's the way my love life mirrors in a fashion:
Sometimes quiet and cosy, past a night of passion.
Sometimes it's a chasing thrill when the evening's going well,
Sometimes recuperating and relaxing for a spell.
Sometimes there's an argument when eyeing up another;
Then I find an even keel and go and visit Mother!

SPECIAL EMBLEM

I watched our standard flutter gently in the breeze,
Saw the duty bugler positioned there at ease.
Soon, then, at attention, everyone was still,
Then I heard the bugle sound and felt a sudden chill.

It's a very special emblem our standard-bearer carries,
Borne aloft with deference where good men meet at rallies.
Gathered in a meeting place in homage to our dead,
It represents raw courage on oceans far widespread.

Dipped in hushed remembrance while standing on parade,
In unison with last post or 'sunset', when it's played,
Reflecting on our brothers at the bottom of the sea,
The unmarked tomb of mariners – freedom is not free.

Worn upon our merchant ships not only when we muster,
It's the mark of British seamen, who call it our red duster.
Sometimes at a funeral it makes a coffin shroud –
A final sad reminder that a veteran's served us proud.

For centuries it's been displayed – time has not forgot
When nobly then it sailed with us into the shell and shot.
I watched our ensign flutter gently in the breeze,
And wiped away a tear when the bugler stood at ease.

Inspired by "Wings" Barry – MNA standard-bearer.

SPIKE AND FID

A sailor born, a sailor bred,
A tough shellback was our man Fred.
His favourite job stood him apart –
Expert splicing was his art.

Rope or wire it didn't matter,
Though 'tis said he chose the latter.
He wormed and parcelled with the lay –
A perfect job in every way.

Serving tight with marline spun,
Grinning proud when all was done,
Alas one night he died in bed –
No more tucks for dear old Fred.

At his graveside stood his wife;
Thought perhaps he'd miss his knife,
Unscrewed then his coffin lid,
Then added too his spike and fid.

TANKER JOE'S

There was a large log cabin down on the River Plate,
Frequented there by tanker men – at a steady rate.
It was famous for its revelry, as every sailor knows,
On the coast of Argentine – and they called it Tanker Joe's.

The oil berths were far away from the mainstream of the town;
The only socialising was in this cabin painted brown.
Inside the barred-up windows with the curtains hung by cords
Were basic chairs and tables, with dust across the boards.

No shortage but of beer and rum, and shelter from the sun,
And local steaks so juicy in a fresh-baked country bun.
Motley crews assembled, with wages there to burn,
Each man at his table – there to take his turn.

These tough men were sailors, and firemen from below,
Many short of schooling and their education low;
But when it came to ballads and other verse in force,
So able was their talent it showed much fine resource.

One by one they took the floor and gave us their rendition
(Some of them were worse for wear, but most in good condition).
There wasn't any music – the words were spoke in hush,
The audience respectful, emotions turned to mush.

With plenty of encouragement they spoke their party word –
It was so very wonderful – the best you've ever heard:
'Maggie May', 'Bull De Mare' and 'The Lady That's Known as Lou',
Also Rudyard Kipling and tales from Miller too.

'From Flanders Fields Where Poppies Blow' was there among the first,
And 'Ship Me East of Suez, Where a Man Can Raise a Thirst',
Titanic verse, John Masefield, and the Bard's great works as well,
'Sam Magee from Tennessee', and 'The Tale of Eskimo Nell'.

Some things you don't forget, and this was one event
Etched into my memory the summer day I spent
Among shellbacks hard as diamonds, who opened up their souls
When stood upon the trestle, acting out their roles.

These mariners of England filled my heart with pride,
When I was a young man with these men by my side.
Innocent as choirboys, they recited favourite prose.
I well remember that day – down at Tanker Joe's.

TANKERMEN

If once you were a tanker man you recall those torrid days
Of seamen at their best and worst in so many ways.
You steamed those tankers up the gulf to where the deserts meet,
To load the oil in Aberdan shimmering in the heat.

You sailed 'em up the Red Sea or Maracaibo lakes,
Or out the port of Galveston in the Southern States.
You may have worked for Esso or the British tanker fleet,
The tramps of John I. Jacobs or the T 2's once elite.

With no domestic fridge, and air scoops made from drums,
Jaspers feeding nightly on old discarded crumbs,
A saucer for the butter, for it melted right away,
Flying fish upon the deck at the dawn of day.

Tanker men were 'nutters' in mariners' folklore,
Imprisoned in an 'oil can' and rarely went ashore,
So it wasn't so surprising they were characters or quaint.
Eccentric were the pump men – as teetotallers they ain't!

You'll not forget cleaning tanks by 'Butterworth' or 'pigs',
The daily tot of welcome rum and duty-free the cigs,
But tanker men were seamen and knew the ruddy score,
Convinced the truly mad men were them that toiled ashore.

ST STEPHEN'S WINDOW

There's a holy place in Bristol – St Stephen's it is known,
One time called the Harbour Church, for it stands within the zone
Abeam of Bristol's centre, where clippers used to moor
When the bustling river once lapped upon its door.

There is now a stained-glass window facing to the south
To honour local seamen that sailed from Avon's mouth,
Depicting the red ensign, plus the navy blue,
Below the merchant-navy crown and the reef knot too.

You may glance to heaven as you intone a prayer,
Perchance to see this tribute to seamen everywhere,
To remind us of all souls that braved their life at sea,
And those reluctant heroes that died for you and me.

TELL THE CHILDREN

A special breed of men, my friend, a special breed of men –
I'm talking of the convoys and remember once again
Seventy years have passed, proving what we owe.
Our debt is all the greater from all those years ago.

Our mariners endured, intrepid and low-paid;
With stubborn sense of purpose carried on their trade.
Still they served our country, sailing there and back,
Hauling vital cargoes in times that looked so black.

These doughty merchant seamen knew their cruel fate,
If struck by cunning sea wolves lurking there in wait.
If they lived to tell their story and strived to stay afloat,
They struggled on with hardships aboard an open boat.

Life goes on, of course – we age, and youngsters grow.
Ask them about the convoys – find out what they know.
Show them our red duster, explain our island race,
Shed light upon the Nelson touch and put the seaman's case.

Spell out the wartime rations and shortage of supplies,
Clarify the fight they had, risking of their lives.
Tell them of the oceans and lifelines to supply –
Our children have their freedom and should know the reason why.

THE CENOTAPH

The Cenotaph calls and England expects
Our people and public to pay our respects.
Agents of forces are first in the queue
To place on the step where garlands are due.

The army the navy and Royal Air Force –
A trio together – the Legion endorse,
Upright and firm on Remembrance Day,
Two minutes' silence the regular way.

The fourth service too must share in first laying –
Clear is the reason that shouldn't need saying.
Then four in a line step back and salute
When resting the wreaths in solemn tribute.

Our merchant navy should simply be there
For giving a life at sea anywhere.
All who served we need to remember,
Equal as heroes this day in November.

THE BUZZ BOMB CAFÉ

After the war in Antwerp – where houses were bombed to rubble –
There stood a single café that managed to keep out of trouble.

In one square mile of city, among buildings razed to the ground,
The Buzz Bomb was open for business – the foundations and
structure were sound.

In acres and acres of wasteland it stood like a beacon to men;
Often I thought it was lucky – so I went there now and again.

THE COAL-SCUTTLE BRIGADE

The war was on our doorstep; the Germans sent us hell,
With their mines and bombers – torpedo boats as well.
Through the E-boat Alley, our colliers braved the way,
Steaming round to London, mostly every day.

They came in coastal convoys from seaports in the north;
Vital coal the cargo – from Tyneside and the Forth,
Providing crucial energy for city and the shires,
As well as fuel for railways and domestic fires.

En route to power stations, with jetties on the river,
Thirty thousand tons a week they needed to deliver.
A voyage runs to Fulham and many a southern quay,
Like the one at Brunswick Wharf and pier at Battersea.

Ships sent down from Welsh ports also braved onslaught,
Through the Hellfire Corner, making life so fraught,
Sitting ducks for E-boats from Goodwin Sands to Dover,
Fifteen guns at Cape Gris Nez lobbing shells right over.

Hardy merchant seamen – experienced sea dogs –
Butted 'tween the sandbars in frequent local fogs.
Defiantly they battled on, fought the harsh oppression,
While losses were horrendous in day and night aggression.

Through the wartime years the colliers sailed the coast,
So many killed or injured giving their utmost,
These our unsung heroes of this battle of the sea;
I only hope you southerners enjoyed your cup of tea!

BATTLE OF THE ATLANTIC

In '42 – part through the war – where the longest battle played,
Our lifeline 'cross the ocean in crucial balance swayed.
Nine thousand men, five million tons, never made it home –
This appalling tally in that twelve months alone.

There was no place to hide in a floating steel abode;
The Hun had found and cracked it – our secret navy code,
They lay across our bow – they knew whereof our route –
Loaded up with tin fish waiting there to shoot.

An order spoke from Hitler to Dönitz and his crew:
'Sink the ships and lifeboats – kill survivors too.'
These infernal words to his U-boats went:
'Rescue none – leave none afloat,' the ghastly message sent.

Dauntless merchant seamen sailed and scorned their fear.
For weeks on end they persevered – vicious death was near –
Slow and easy targets for the Kriegsmarine,
Launching their torpedoes in day and night routine.

These lethal hungry wolf packs, lurking out of sight,
Delivered mortal damage in this underhanded fight.
Convoys crossed the 'black pit' beyond the reach of planes,
Contending with the enemy and awesome hurricanes.

Our mariners endured – steaming through hell's gate,
Powerless and helpless, to know their own ship's fate.
Difficult and dangerous, also poorly paid,
With stubborn sense of purpose they carried on their trade.

In '43, eventually, the tide was slowly turned –
Brave escorts grew formidable with tactic lessons learned,
Aircraft stretched from Iceland flying to the hilt,
Long-range Liberators with radar newly built.

Canadians and Yanks toiled to aid us through,
Supporting our red duster and turning of the screw.
All we have of freedom that we use or know,
Seamen helped to bring it, many years ago.

THE BOSUN

The Bosun's legs were damaged, swollen black and blue;
Chief Steward quite bewildered, not sure what to do.
Consulting then the Captain, they studied up the guide
(A special one for masters to take advice inside).

This captain's medical guide covers all the ills,
Though instructions are ambiguous for serving drugs and pills.
There's cures for mental illness, scalds and having babies,
Plus fevers, burns, athlete's foot, drugs, alcohol and rabies.

The Captain was quite practised, his duty wouldn't shun,
Reckoned he had cracked it, knew what must be done.
They had sailed from Argentina, the weather hot and red.
Said the right thing for the Bosun was cool him in his bed.

'Stack his legs with frozen cubes' was order to his crew –
All hands mostly happy now, knowing what to do.
The chippy made a special box to fit this man precise,
Shoved the Bosun's limbs in, then filled it up with ice.

The chief worked hard with spanners to keep the fridges purring,
Night and day maintained away to make the frost occurring.
Steaming through the tropics they looked after him with pride,
Chilling down the Bosun on his scorching ocean ride.

He lay there in a stupor as he followed this routine
Of frequent shots of rum while piling ice between.
They finally reached Cape Verde and put the man ashore.
Bunkered then with booze and fuel, sailed again once more.

Most mariners are hardy – go through life with ease,
Not troubled much with ailments or tropical disease,
Till the ship received a cable saying, '*Bad news I'm afraid:
Your man expired of frostbite . . . when ninety in the shade.*'

THE BUGLER

Our Bill played the bugle, our Bill played last post,
Bill came through the Great War – luckier than most.
Lance Corporal William Turner – his proper name, you see –
Fought there in the trenches with Highland Infantry.

Playing over battlefields on sodden mud landscapes,
He sounded off at burials – frequently his mates.
Bill was knocked about a bit by one exploding shell –
The same that killed his general, so played at his as well.

Later on in '83 he returned nearby once more,
Bringing back his bugle – the one he played before.
Standing at the cemeteries with tearful shining eyes,
He paid respect to colleagues – his battalion guys.

Now this year his daughter – Peggy Tolfree – came
With her dad's old bugle, turning out again
To visit battle graveyards and the Menin Gate,
Where you'll hear the last post for men who met their fate.

There is a certain romance between a bugler's call
And a stirring memory that people may recall –
A rallying cry or death knell, whatever it may be,
It's men like William Turner that bring it home to me.

November 2004.

134

THE CALL OF THE SEA

In our island nation, within the shores of the free,
There is salt in the veins of our kinfolk and lust for life at sea.
Many seamen at home that swallowed the anchor back then,
Time and again have the urge to pack their bags once again.

For they sailed out east through the Suez to the far-off Indian shore,
Or steamed off west with cargoes to docks like Baltimore,
North in Arctic weather through the snow and the ice,
Or southern climes with palm trees and musky smell of the spice.

They kept a watch from the fo'c'sle, an eye on the rise of the moon,
Or daylight trick at the helm till eight bells struck at noon.
Sights they took with a sextant, then pencilled a fix on the chart,
Or mothered the engines all constant, attending every part.

They heard the banshee screaming of storms sent over the deep,
Accustomed hard to seafaring, nursing the vessel's keep,
Taking their fun and their fancy in ports wherever found,
Perhaps tattoos of a sailing ship inscribed with 'Homeward-Bound'.

They travelled the globe for months at a time over the ocean foam,
Friendships forged of the lasting kind with men destined to roam.
Still the life of a rover sometimes beckons to me –
I reckon it's salt in the veins, and the call of the sea.

THE COLLISION OF THE SS *CONNEMARA* AND SS *RETRIEVER*

Picture the awful conditions on entering Carlingford Lough –
A collier named *Retriever* was heading for Newry Dock.
Wild was that night in November – she was pitching and taking a roll,
Sheering hard and sluggish with a shifting cargo of coal.

Beyond the bar was a channel – a cut less than two cables wide –
A dodgy place to be passing in storm-force squalls and the tide.
Because of the fear of U-boats, her lights were suitably dimmed
As she battled to enter the channel pummelled by sea and the wind.

The SS *Connemara*, steaming out for Holyhead –
With little room for manoeuvre, they discerned each other with dread.
Recently sailing from Greenore, she too with lights obscured,
With passengers including young women and children also on board.

Her engine astern too late, the *Retriever* went on to collide –
The collier struck the steamer, her bow slicing open her side,
The *Connemara*, her boilers exploding, sank in quick disarray;
The *Retriever*, with her bows stove in, sunk just fathoms away.

Loss of life was heavy – ninety-three the score,
Counting up the cost next day where bodies washed ashore.
A graveyard in Kilkeel holds a memorial stone
To recall this night of disaster when a single survivor went home.

Atrocious weather the reason, 100 years ago,
But 'tis right to remind us all, and for people to know
It's not always a favourable tide whenever you sail from the quay,
Or conditions settled and peaceful when cast off and sailing the sea.

2016

On 3 November 1916 a fateful collision occurred between the SS Retriever *(a collier of 483 tons, with a cargo of coal from Garston and a crew of nine) and the SS* Connemara *(a twin-screw steamer, 272 feet long and 1,100 tons gross) in hurricane-force winds, mountainous seas and an eight-knot tide at the entrance to Carlingford Lough. The number of lives reported lost was between ninety-three and ninety-seven.*

THE SS *CATO*'S CREW

Brave coasting men of the *Cato*
Served on a Bristol line,
Sailed and did their duty
Under the red ensign.
They bore the brunt
On the Channel front
When hitting a German mine.

THE SS *CATO*

Remember men of the coastal trade,
Especially the *Cato*'s crew.
Seamen fine of a Bristol line –
They earned the credit due.

A special breed of men, they sailed the short sea routes,
Without a navy escort or anything that shoots,
Hardy blokes and able, intrepid to the core,
Regardless of the perils lurking in the war.

Steaming home from Dublin, the *Cato* struck a mine,
Planted there a week before by U-boat *29*.
Straight away she blew up and sank there in the tide.
Of fifteen men aboard, only two survived.

She'd come to grief off Nash Point during that foul day –
Her cargo holds with Irish stout began to break away.
Many barrels of freight (of 400 tons in all)
Beached along the coast from Cardiff to Porthcawl.

She was known as the Guinness Wreck by locals on the shore,
And provided drinking sessions – according to folklore.
Perhaps the crew of the *Cato* did not die in vain –
By telling of this story, we remember them again.

They could not help the Guinness Wreck – it was a German flaw.
The cargo *was* delivered – but through a Welshman's door!

THE *CITY OF ADELAIDE*

Forgotten on a slipway at Irvine, near the Clyde,
Lies a legend of a sailing ship, her timbers grey and dried.
Older than the *Cutty Sark*, she'll soon be lost forever
Unless there is the funding with pretty strong endeavour.

She's a clipper from the early days of perfect ship design
That voyaged to Australia and set a record time.
Under first-class seamanship, by the Captain's hand,
She carried out the emigrants who stocked that pleasant land.

One-quarter million people in those southern spheres
Can trace their roots to passages in those early years.
Aboard this marvellous clipper their forebears travelled out
Through the roaring forties sailing east about.

Built in '64 by a man named William Pile,
Launching her from Sunderland in the British Isle.
Then twenty-three long voyages, returning round the Horn,
Driven by the fickle wind and seamen's hearty brawn.

Composite of iron frame with hardy elm and oak,
Cabins for the colonists, special and bespoke.
In the name of preservation and history maritime,
It's worthy of a mention if only here in a rhyme.

Sadly now she's overlooked, an icon of the past
Crying out for refit and rigging of her masts.
She could be overhauled again to remind us of the time
When brave descendants ventured out and she was in her prime.

THE CREM

"Farewell now," our padre says to the coffin by his side.
Alas another mariner has crossed the bar and died.
Once he was a seaman in a calling like no other,
With an understanding to us he was a brother.

The padre singles out the man, below an ensign red,
Speaks of deeds with humour about the life he'd led,
Of the hard and best times when he was young at sea,
Till finally ashore to raise a family.

Sent off by fellow seamen – from deep-sea or the coast –
Perhaps a tape recording rendering last post.
The 'star turn' in the coffin does not mind at all,
Because he knew beforehand what later might befall.

Kinfolk in the for'ard pews paying last respects,
Our veterans in blazers wondering if they're next.
Words about the evening star and peril on the sea,
Surmising I'll be happy when Father Time calls me.

We attend with deference the funerals of our peers,
Especially with our padre evoking laughs and tears.
It's sad, I know, we'll miss them so, but a voyage too must end;
We're here to bid farewell to a colleague and a friend.

August 2017

D-DAY ARMADA: OPERATION NEPTUNE

Rank after relentless rank they came,
Facing guns, bombs and flame,
Six thousand craft, ten lanes wide,
Advancing in the ripping tide.

Seven hundred warships too,
Armed and set with a job to do.
Fast minesweepers at the van,
Fighter squadrons weaved and ran.

Twenty miles across the beam,
The greatest convoy ever seen –
Endless columns of surging craft,
Landing ships with shallow draft.

Liners, ferries packed with troops,
Attack transports, army groups.
Barrage balloons on display
Spread across this vast array.

Red Cross vessels, laden tankers,
Ancient tubs missing anchors.
Coastguard cutters, motor boats
Painted out in grey topcoats.

Channel steamers out from Dover,
Modern freighters steaming over,
Winking lights as Morse is spoke,
Rusty coasters belching smoke.

Swarms of tugs, rolling tramps
Packed with stores, guns and tanks.
They sailed this day for liberty
To crush the foe and set us free.

THE FREEDOM OF OUR CITY

The freedom of our land, men, the freedom of our land;
Now we think of doughty men and how you made a stand.
Our country really needed you when called on to defend –
It's that you fought and died for till the bitter end.

The freedom of our seas, boys, the freedom of our seas;
You carried on your duty, boys, sailing from the quays.
Ranging round the world in peace, also in the wars,
You reluctant heroes hauled succour to our shores.

The freedom of our city, lads, the freedom of our city,
For you merchant-navy lads who brought prosperity
In Bristol's recognition – and at the people's bid,
Take honour from our citizens recalling what you did.

*On the merchant navy being granted the freedom of the City of
Bristol, July 2002.*

THE FO'C'SLE OF THE DEAD

I will tell you of a story that is waiting to be told –
A yarn about a graveyard for mariners of old,
Placed in San Francisco, lost to one and all,
Behind abandoned buildings with graffiti on the wall.

In a little valley, ringed around with trees,
By an old presidio that crumbled to its knees,
A merchant-navy hospital long ago once stood,
With a cemetery well hidden and 'gravestones' made of wood.

The place was just abandoned and left there to its fate,
Marked faintly on the map as 'landfill number eight',
A parking lot on one corner making lots of cover,
A tennis court spread across making up another.

An archaeologist, interested, poking with a hoe
Discovered, under weeds, headstones in a row.
Excavations from a missile site had covered up the place,
With many feet of debris adding to disgrace.

Probing ever further they found this eerie plot:
Six hundred graves of seamen – and more, as like as not.
These crewmen of sailing ships entered Frisco Bay –
Hard labour and TB meant they never sailed away.

Many died when they were young as old records show –
The latest men interred there ninety years ago.
All were merchant mariners, but no one seemed to care.
Several plots were unmarked and rubbish dumped on there.

A suitable memorial will be placed upon the site,
Explaining to the public the pauper seamen's plight.
They will not be exhumed, powers that be have said –
There they will remain in the Fo'c'sle of the Dead.

October 2008

Joe Earl, 1957.

Able seaman on MV Cato, *Antwerp, 1962.*

Able seaman, MV Cato.

First mate on MV Milo, *1965.*

Tasmania Star, *New Zealand, 1961.*

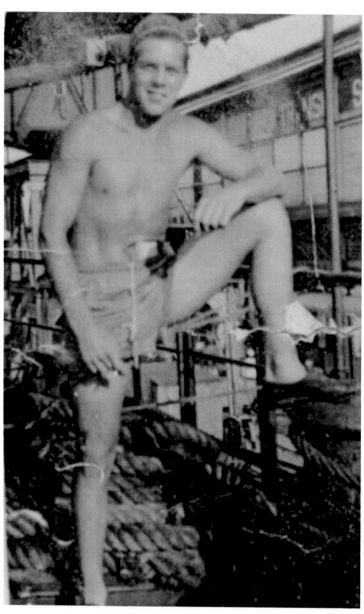

John Earl, the author's brother.

Dry Dock, MV Echo.

MV Apollo *anchored in Walton Bay, 1975.*

On leave, 1957.

The Indefatigable *School Band.*

Indefatigable *training ship.*

Under the bow – Point Gilbert.

On leave from Indefatigable, *Caernarvon Castle.*

Receiving the Merchant Navy Medal from Lord West, 2009.

Sussex Trader, *1961*.

Tremayne, *1959.*

The Menai Straits – where we 'messed about in boats'.

THE HALF-MARATHON RUNNER

Half a marathon – I've done it before.
I'm trying again to better my score.
It's not about winning or glory or wealth,
Nor really a trip to rack up my health.

Just like a convoy heading for port,
The journey is long, conditions are fraught.
The battle with hurt I have to fight through,
Encouraged by words from some of the crew.

Some stragglers I'm passing, exhausted their fuel –
A pity for them, but the voyage is cruel.
Can't stop to help them – I must carry on,
Plodding and heaving and pounding along.

Leaving the debris and carnage behind,
I'm pressing on – I've made up my mind.
My rate of knots is slightly below,
But still hope to make it sans tugs or a tow.

The bunting is out – I've made it all right,
Though running repairs will take me all night.
Sponsors have paid and veterans will say,
"Well done, old timer – you cracked it today."

October 2014

Inspired by Doug May, winner of the Bristol Half Marathon (13.1 miles), 21 September 2014.

The EXPLOSION OF THE SS *FORT STIKINE*

The *Fort Stikine*, a coal-burner, was built in '42,
Managed by the Port Line with a hardy crew,
Canadian built – a Liberty ship – she sailed from Birkenhead,
Joining with a convoy to Gibraltar then Port Said.

Her discharging port was Bombay in February '44,
Risking many perils to reach there in the war.
Her cargo was explosives stowed within the hold,
Plus six score of ingots – each two stone of gold.

A thousand drums of oil with cotton underlaid,
Volatile munitions of highly dangerous grade;
Scrap iron too was plentiful loaded down below –
The makings of a bomb, then, waiting there to blow.

At her berth in Bombay, with many ships about,
Fear was raised on board when someone gave a shout.
A fire took hold so quickly, which rapid took a grip –
Discretion used to scarper and abandon ship.

An explosion sent her boiler five cables' lengths away –
Many nearby vessels were sunk or scrapped that day.
Shells, gold bars and oil drums with several bits of mast,
Flaming bales of cotton hurled up with the blast.

Shanties of the local slums turned kindling at a stroke –
Three days to douse the fires underneath the smoke.
Thousands killed or wounded emanating from
The cargo of a freighter that turned into a bomb.

Emergency response teams needed three days to control the fire. Eight thousand men took seven months to remove the 500,000 tons of debris that the SS Fort Stikine *scattered when she exploded, and to repair the damage her explosion did to the docks. Official records place the death toll at 740 – 476 of whom were military personnel. Eighteen hundred people were injured as a result of the explosion, and a total of twenty-seven vessels were sunk or damaged in the docks.*

The docks explosion was the result of a series of mistakes and miscalculations on the part of everyone involved. The Number 2 hold of the SS Fort Stikine *contained 769 tons of raw cotton, timber and scrap iron. The compartment above this contained leaking drums of oil, 124 bars of gold, and 168 tons of category-A explosives. Altogether three of the SS* Fort Stikine's *five holds contained a combination of highly flammable raw cotton, sensitive explosives and fuel. Together these would prove to be a deadly mix.*

THE FAN DANCER

"Are you, sir, an old sailor man gazing out to sea?"
"I was, young sir, a sailor man. What do you want of me?"
"Is it true that in the old days you did sail easterly?"
"Indeed I did. Let's find a seat, then listen close to me."
"I've heard that in the Orient things aren't quite the same."
"To answer you I need a drink – a large one is my aim."
"Are you going to tell me now of the ladies of Japan?"
"Aye, this whisky's good, so thanks, and cheers to you, young man.

"There's strange things done in the rising sun and one of them's no lie:
The ladies' bits flow east and west, the same way as their eye.
I do know that, but I'll tell you flat of the time I was taken in,
In a port called Yokohama in a place of red-light sin,
There I met a maiden – she wore a green kimono,
She was a thing of beauty, her name was Sidjeko.
I ardently pursued her and watched her sexy dance.
As she twirled around with feathered fans I prayed I had a chance.

"My mates all agreed with me and did not cast a slur.
Such grace and charm she had as I fell in love with her.
I had found my lass divine – my brain was in a whirl,
My Oriental dancer, my shapely, perfect girl,
Healthy, witching, wise, with loveliness serene.
Proud I was to win this prize, half angel and half queen,
I'd seen the world and many girls though not yet twenty-four;
My future clear I could settle near this lady I adore.

"I could see she fell for me, was not the least bit haughty,
So jumped with glee and took her home, my thoughts a little naughty.
She performed for me quite privately, she really turned me on;
What happened next defies belief with total cover gone.
She danced and teased until the end, then jettisoned her fan.
Well, blow me down – I never guessed – the lady was a man!
I could not believe it – my mind was in a fog.
So I upped and ran – just scarpered like a robber's dog.

"Later, in the bar, my mind in slow reflection,
I asked about my dancer – the one I popped the question.
By night I found she pranced around near naked as Godiva;
By day he ran the local tram – I'm told he was the driver.
There's strange things done in the rising sun, but, lad, you must remember,
If you fall for an Oriental, be sure to check the gender.
An' it's wise to leave the lights on when in your sexual prime,
Or you may have a shock by a man in a frock and waste your drinking time."

THE LIBERTY SHIPS

Thompson built a welded ship up at Sunderland –
Ten thousand tons she carried, and structure simply planned.
When the U-boat war broke out we had to hold the line,
But cargo ships were sinking in that horrendous time.

So using modern methods he mass-produced some more.
'*Empire*' was the prefix of every name they bore.
There was the *Empire Ranger* and the *Empire Deer*
Among the names of many launched there on the Wear.

She was called an ugly duckling, dressed in wartime grey;
Holds were four in number and flush decks all the way;
Eleven knots her foremost speed, armed with basic guns,
But crucial to our lifeline on dangerous convoy runs.

Copied by our Allies, they built 'em in the States,
And named them after heroes – of the nation's 'greats',
Like the *William Hooper*, *Dan Boone* or *Joseph Meek* –
Delivered from the shipyards, several every week.

They built them too in Canada, but named them after parks.
Canadians that manned them trained and then embarked.
Mount Pleasant Park and *Jasper Park* sadly met their fate,
Shattered by the enemy while steaming with their freight.

British crews that joined them had a different name,
Sailing in the 'Fort' boats constructed just the same.
Fort Bedford and *Fort Brandon* just two of plenty more
That carried precious cargoes from shore to distant shore.

Later on the 'Victory' ships came on to the scene,
Longer and much faster and broader in the beam.
They called them after cities like the *Bedford Victory*,
All crewed by unsung heroes that fought the war at sea.

April 2010

The President had told the country that these ships would bring liberty to Europe. From then on, they were known as Liberty ships. It was said during the war that if a Liberty ship delivered its cargo but once, it paid for itself.

Approximately 2,742 Liberty ships were built, and 200 of them were sunk.

THE LAST REUNION: SHIPS

You've heard of Para Handy and his puffer, *Vital Spark*;
Of course you know of Noah and the grounding of his Ark.
All vessels have a life and time, with natural will and ways,
Rolling and a-pitching when steaming through the waves.

You may ask the veterans in Liverpool's fair city,
Gathered here in final year to a band's last ditty.
Time has gone, but memory's long while shellbacks are alive –
They'll speak of ships on danger trips that helped them to survive.

Some craft faced mortality in Western Ocean's roar,
Waiting death from U-boats in that cruel and mighty war,
Till the deadly tin fish met them on the flanks
Of liners and the escorts, the tankers and the tramps.

Some torpedoed in their prime, plates all ripped and tearing;
Other ones grew old and carried on seafaring.
They died a death or lived a life, maybe badly mauled,
Flying our red duster wherever duty called.

From the wallowing rusty bucket to the liner up ahead,
Someone somewhere loved 'em with grieving eyes so red.
We do remember those ships that steamed along in lines.
They saved our land when needed, in dire and desperate times.

After sterling service and life that's very hard,
Her decks and loosened rivets met the breaker's yard.
They weathered all the storms – now just cast aside,
But, like the men that manned 'em, bless 'em all with pride.

There is no stone on a ship's big tomb –
Just names marked down in the Admiral's room.
Their only cross on a chart prostrate,
A pencilled fix to point their fate.

THE LOOKOUT ON A RUSSIAN-CONVOY SHIP

You were mighty cold on the Russian Arctic run
When stationed there as lookout at night without the sun,
Blurring of the vision by buffeting of winds,
Tears of ice down the cheeks while peering through the bins.

Eyelashes were frozen, icing up together,
Breaking off so painfully when melting out of weather.
Inhaling brought such agony in sub-nothing air;
On top of that the enemy, who could be anywhere.

Brutal wild conditions black as any caves;
Fog or driving snow and mountainous the waves.
Bully beef as main course, hot drink hard to get,
Accommodation dripping and clothes were sodden wet.

Possibly you suffered grief by witnessing the end
Of companion ships in convoy or a fellow friend.
No asylum either if arriving outward-bound,
Beset by bombs and strafing in constant battleground.

They did not think of medals on that morale-sapping trip,
Just carried out their duties in wartime's surly grip.
Many of those journeys made a sacrifice,
With cargoes, ships and seamen paying of the price.

THE MEN WHO MISSED THE TIDE

I was not born till '41 – I wasn't at the fore,
But later on I sailed with men who told me what they saw.
There never was a phoney war for the merchant men at sea,
Especially in the early years – with two men lost from three.
Sitting ducks for E-boats and explosives in Bomb Alley,
An easy moving target from engine room to galley.

They were blown from burning ships, torpedoed by the Hun,
Or victims of atrocity shot by a Nippon gun.
Plenty perished in lifeboats; many gave the sharks a feast.
Still pretty much defenceless, the ships rolled west and east.
They sailed north in Russian convoys, braved the ice and foe,
Lived in hell conditions – and pitching blind in snow.

Some sailed independent – they steamed south on their own,
Perchance to meet the U-boat lurking neath the foam.
Many thousand seamen died risking life at sea.
It was the brave survivors who told me their history.
The lethal mines would sink them, or the tin fish named by some,
Or possibly a Junkers on a mortal bombing run.

Crews foundered in the ocean black or freezing cold,
With mangled steel beneath them and pig iron in the hold.
But if they shunned the enemy, and escaped the heaving slaughter,
Well, they just signed on again and went back to the water.
To the lads that never made it home – to all the men that died –
Wouldn't it be apt to say, "They never made the tide"?

Over forty years I've toiled at sea, aboard all types of craft,
But I doff my cap to those young souls that went and joined a raft.
I'm mighty proud to march for them on the 11th of November –
For this very special breed of men that I for one remember.
I haven't any medals, but I wear my badge with pride
As the bugle sounds the last post for the men who missed the tide.

THE MERCHANT NAVY ASSOCIATION
ALPHABET, BRISTOL

A is attendance when we turn to en masse.
B is for beer – a nice pint of bass.
C is the cash for a tarpaulin muster.
D is devotion to our famous red duster.

E is existence of the friendly warm greeting.
F is for farewell at the end of each meeting.
G is the Gents, where we go to pump ship.
H is for high spirits when off on a trip.

I is the input we get from the boys.
J is for the jokes as old as convoys.
K is for keel to keep even and stable.
L is for leadership from the top table.

M is for memories – there's many of them.
N is for nautical – seafaring men.
O is for old shellbacks now living on land.
P is the parade when we march to the band.

Q is for questions when we'd like to know more.
R is for reply to those on the floor.
S is for the ships that we spent our time on.
T is for our talent that steamed 'em along.

U is the uniform of blazer and tie.
V is for voyage and shouts of "Aye aye."
W is for waterfront with monument and trees.
X is for Xmas we've spent overseas.

Y is for the yarns and the stories we know.
Z is for zest and our get-up-and-go.

THE MERCHANT NAVY

"The merchant navy, with Allied comrades, night and day, in weather fair or foul, faces not only the ordinary perils of the sea, but the sudden assaults of war from beneath the waters or from the sky. Your first task is to bring to port the cargoes vital for us at home and for our armies abroad and we trust your tenacity and resolve to see this stern task through."

Sir Winston Churchill, 1941

"I consider the protection of our trade the most essential service that can be performed."

Admiral Lord Nelson to Captain Benjamin Hallowell, 1804

THE MERMAID

Once I saw a mermaid posing on a rock,
Sexy, pert and curvy, but I'm not trying to shock.
She's often been depicted in photo and green crayon
And sits upon your starboard hand as you enter Copenhagen.

THE MILO
(Bristol Steam Navigation Co. Ltd)

I was mate aboard the *Milo*, sailing out the bay,
From Swansea to old Amsterdam in the usual way,
Pounding in the head sea, with Land's End far ahead,
Laden down with cargo – twelve hundred tons of lead.

Making heavy headway, sou'-west is the course,
In rising swell and winter wind, blowing near storm force.
I can sense the hog and sag, fit to break her back,
Lightning 'tween the squalls an' sporadic thunderclap.

Everything vibrating, she shudders with the shock
(Hope the bolts are holding round the engine block).
There's salt upon the funnel, now as white as snow,
Propeller shaft a-racing and a shambles down below.

Quite normal on a coaster, so plotting closer now,
Toward the Cornish lighthouse two points on the bow.
"Ready now, my shellbacks, your wages soon will earn –
Another half an hour or so, we're primed to make a turn."

The cargo's safe and staying put as violently we roll
(Far worse than normal cargo, like the bulky coal).
Aching body weary now at the break of day,
With quarter seas a-heaving she's steering like a dray.

Now we have the Longships, way abaft the beam,
Looking for the Lizard Point – soon it will be seen.
Jammed against the telegraph, supping mugs of soup,
Jarring all my bones up as she takes one on the poop.

Longing for an hour's kip, no dozing off between
My watch below, but standing by while shipping seas of green.
"Roll and go; pitch and stop" is what all seamen say.
That's a fact as heading east we're shooting past Mount's Bay.

Easing up the Channel, averting other craft,
The lads are cleaning up a bit in the galley aft.
The engines will be nurtured after rack and strain,
For bearing us to other ports – or take us home again.

Steaming past the Goodwin Sands, Dover's out of sight –
We'll have a crack in Amsterdam and take a drink tonight.
I often think of runs like this in my old-age dreams:
My young days on the *Milo* – one of Bristol Steam's.

THE PADDLE STEAMER *BARRY*

Cheers to the pleasure steamer, popular and fast,
With a jaunty rake of funnel and bunting from the mast.
Paddles swooshing easily, foaming as they churn,
Leaving wake ruler-straight, trailing there astern.

Her glossy shining paintwork of red and pearly white,
Flying proud the ensign on halyard whipping tight,
The cheering of the passengers leaning on the rail
And jingle of the telegraph when about to sail.

The fascinating engines steaming hell for leather,
Captain's orders from the bridge open to the weather,
Called upon in wartime years for such sterling work,
Plus helping out the navy and army at Dunkirk.

One such vessel of renown was the PS *Barry*,
Famous in the Great War for troops she had to carry,
Outstanding in Gallipoli and last from Suvla Bay,
Serving at Salonika, toiled in danger's way.

She was built upon the Clyde 100 years ago,
Excursion-fit for passengers on deck and down below.
Registered in Barry – in her early years,
Calling in the channel ports, mooring at the piers.

Ilfracombe or Weston, down to old Minehead,
Burnham and the Mumbles – then home in time for bed.
She gave so many people hours of bracing pleasure,
Merrymaking families enjoying days to treasure.

Later on in '26 she worked our southern climes,
Sailing out of Brighton and Hastings many times;
Then sweeping mines in '41 on a fatal run,
She perished in the North Sea, sunk there by the Hun.

It's right recalling history of South Wales long ago,
Of local crew and seamen sailing to and fro,
For they worked the paddle steamers, giving them their power,
In our favourite waters – from Bristol to the Gower.

The Paddle Steamer Barry *was built for the Barry Railway Company's fleet and sailed on 24 May 1907, before leaving the Clyde to begin her pleasure-steamer career from Barry sailing in Bristol Channel.*

THE PANAMA CANAL MULES

There was many a lad on a tanker, a liner or tramp of the sea
That saved up bread for the 'mules', and one of those lads was me,
Informed by the crew it was routine, and nice to be such a pal,
By hoarding grub for old Dobbin, working the long canal.

For weeks while crossing the ocean, earning a deck boy's pay,
I stored all scraps and loaves there – plenty every day.
Later on, arriving, you could knock me down with a feather,
For it weren't the type of mule with legs and reins of leather.

These beasts had ruddy big engines, a locomotive wide.
The game was up – I knew it: I'd been taken for a ride.
Quick as a flash, in a hurry, I dumped my donkey stores,
Not acting like a lubber or a stranger to these shores.

I pretended I wasn't so stupid, but wise to their childish game,
Patting myself on the back for avoiding terrible shame.
But galley boys and Peggys that fell for the seamen's ruse
Will never forget those mules – and bread they didn't use.

THE MOLLY MOGGS

In all the pubs in all the world singled out for praise,
It's the Molly Moggs in Soho for all the funds they raise,
Specially for our mariners and veterans of war,
And the unsung heroes that struggled at the fore.

On the corner of Old Compton Street this pub's a little gem.
Built in 1700, her pedigree's from then.
Plenty are the bar stools, but not a lot of space.
Hearty entertainment is the highlight of the place.

Some clientele enthral with witty quips so gay,
Bonding all together in their camp and funny way.
They recognise the value of duty to the end,
Selfless with their time and energy they lend.

Famous for its drag shows and fabulous inside,
Historic and important for old London's pride,
Performers are just marvellous, open and sincere,
Collecting for our heroes when punters come for cheer.

Raising cash for brave folk is humble and sublime –
Patrons of the Molly Moggs do it all the time.
This cultured bar is friendly to all of us out there –
Best of all a grand spot for those that really care.

November 2009

THE PEARLY GATES

The Pearly Gates are open wide – there the Captain stands,
Ticking off a lengthy roll at the passing of all hands.
He does not look for plaster saints or someone he has missed –
He's searching for brave mariners further down the list.

Life at sea was fraught enough before the war began,
Though ship's routine was normal and fair to every man.
Then the conflict started – the hell began and how!
Peace was really shattered when a mine blew off the bow.

They carried vital cargoes for us to fight the foe,
Across the rolling oceans, transporting to and fro.
It wasn't quite so placid when a Junkers bombed the deck,
Or jumping in the briny with a lifebelt round the neck.

They also sailed on 'buckets' – in tramps that's most corrosion.
What was worse and more diverse was suffering from explosion.
They could man up any craft, from liners to a barque,
But scrambled to a life raft when torpedoes found their mark.

In convoys or alone – where defence was mighty thin –
They were striving for survival when the plates were crumpled in,
Seamen knew the hazards, like storms and drifting fog,
But not a German raider with a shellfire monologue.

When they entered heaven the Master made his marks,
By the names of merchant men who shared the sea with sharks.
He did not query good or bad – amiss or mainly sober –
But praised them for the lives they gave, ere the war was over.

When you see the albatross patrol the southern climes,
It's said they bear the sailor souls of those heroic times,
Flying free and happily where no one shoots 'em down,
Soaring to eternity – nevermore to drown.

THE PLAQUE

Stand by this dedication on Bristol's old Welsh Back,
Where seamen and their families are there to set a plaque
Pertaining to all youngsters that gave their life at sea.
Those plucky unsung heroes sailed for you and me.

Greater than 500 boys were sent to Neptune's floor –
Seventeenth birthdays never met, lost for evermore.
They helped sustain our lifelines in dark and violent times,
Facing bombs and U-boats as well as floating mines.

They came from many seaports and towns from in between –
Our nation's youngest mariners, fighting fit and keen,
Committed to adventure with crews wherein they fit,
While barely out of school or hardy training ship.

Life at sea was tough enough with hazards every quarter,
But conflict with the enemy made hell upon the water.
Precious to their shipmates, and loved ones all at home,
They carried out their duties while steaming o'er the foam.

We owe a debt of gratitude to all our merchant men,
But today a special tribute is paid to boys like them.
Yes, we will remember by the fixing of a plaque,
Hard by our seamen's monument, enduring on Welsh Back.

February 2017

THE PURTON EIGHTY-ONE

On one long edge of grassy bank the canal lies full and still.
The river swirls on t'other side with certain back and fill.
Strewn about like skeletons only half interred
Are ghostly hulks of vessels, mostly undisturbed.

All the small ships mentioned with fond poetic glow
Were beached along this Severn stretch many years ago,
The steel barge *River Falcon* near a former bridge,
And *Tirley* fully buried, beneath a muddy ridge.

A section of the *Jonadab* poking out of spoil,
Components of the *Higre* most buried in the soil,
The foredeck of the *Edith* showing up in turn,
The name of *Severn Collier* remaining on her stern.

Cross-bracing of the *New Dispatch* with evidence of fire,
The transom of the *Harriett* resting in the mire,
The haunted *Britton Ferry* with sternpost pointing out,
Timbers left of *Monarch* mouldering there throughout.

There is the wooden *Abbey* where sodden turf is growing,
Gunwale of the *Ada*, her iron knees still showing,
The *Shamrock* and *Conveyer* not a step too far,
From the bow of *Rockby* and the lighter *J & AR*.

Stern part of the *Petrus*, a workhorse of her time,
Bow and stern of *Huntley* and *Dursley* there in line;
Newark and *Britannia* are making up the ranks;
Marriett and *Voltaic* are elsewhere on the banks.

Remnants of the *Orby* once the *Island Maid*,
Cemented hulls of FCBs from the river trade,
The Irish *Kathleen Ellen*, of gun and smuggling fame,
Embedded deep with ketches and *Selina Jane*.

There is *Envoy* and the *Painswick* with the *Mary Anne*,
Iron rings and fairleads through where the moorings ran,
The port side of the *Barry* protruding through the grass,
And the schooner *Sally* where vandals nicked the brass.

Eighty-one the number catalogued so far –
Some names of them forgotten since they crossed the bar.
A graveyard, then, of mystery and maritime old bones,
Ensconced within a riverbank of mounting mud and stones.

THE RECIPE FOR LIFE

There are many things a man may learn to lead a happy life,
To help him through those troubled times or evicted by his wife.
The first thing to ascertain – apart from not to worry,
Keeping fit and going strong – is how to make a curry.

An' if you're on your own, and think it's awful tough,
Relax and get the pot on – I think you've moped enough.
Have a go at Madras – it's fever, spice and fun.
It'll teach you independence – will do you good, my son.

First you need a big pan and sit it on to stew,
A few cans of tomatoes – no salt, that's bad for you.
Add a pack of Chinese veg and a few pounds of minced beef –
That will be the basis of a curry 'yond belief.

You may also add some mushrooms and onions when beginning –
It helps to fight the battle of life, especially if you're winning.
A wondrous dish all through the day, or perhaps a little later.
Another way to top it up – chuck in a few potater.

If a lady friend comes home with you, serve repast with pride –
Better then with korma, gentler there inside.
After one or two days, when the pan is getting low,
Add a couple of hard-boiled eggs and keep it on the go.

Never clean the pan out – you must keep its spicy flavour.
Just add what you started with – a meal that's one to savour,
I have tasted curries from Walsall to Bombay,
But I've rarely eaten better than the one at home today.

In single-life contentment I'm never going back.
I'm happier scoffing curry with pints of applejack.
It tightens up your sinews, and that can be quite handy –
Also keeps you virile, and it makes me so damn randy.

Ain't life a bitch!

THE RED ENSIGN

On all the seas and rivers where British seamen go,
From the tropics to the edges of where the icebergs grow,
You will see the ruddy bunting of bright or smoky red –
It's our merchant-navy ensign flying overhead.

Many an eye has danced at our banner flying true;
Our hearts and souls are British, and our colours too.
Whipping in defiance when white waves are below,
It flew above the vanquished and defeated foe.

No one should prevent us from hoisting it by day.
Since 1824 its prominence held sway,
Either flying in the breeze when trading near and far
Or draped upon a coffin when a seaman's crossed the bar.

It's more than just a symbol of a nation brave and free –
Not only just an emblem proclaiming liberty –
For the showing of our duster from gaff or lofty spar
Sets pride among our mariners, no matter where they are.

THE SS *DAYBREAK*

Nineteen seventeen it was – during perilous days –
The freighter SS *Daybreak*, loaded deep with maize,
Steamed along on Christmas Eve near the Southern Rock,
Off the coast of County Down abeam of Strangford Lough.
No notice or forewarning, a torpedo found its mark –
It came and blew the nose right off, plunging all in dark.
The vessel's screw rotating during its descent,
Her boilers then exploding as underneath they went.

U-boat *87* had loosed her lethal load,
To meet this helpless target on a winter's ocean road.
One and twenty brave men – the total of her crew –
Murdered in the Irish Sea by folk they never knew.
It was seen by witnesses, or perhaps we'd never know
What occurred to brave men dragged down far below,
Entombed there now forever, thirty fathoms deep,
Akin to unsung mariners in Davy Jones's keep.

THE SS *ROBIN*

Launched in 1890, the *Robin*'s fine design
Made this old steam coaster a classic of her time.
She rolled and navigated around our coast for years,
Driven by her engines and doughty engineers.

Replacing brigs and schooners, she plied her salty trade,
Four hundred tons or more on a voyage made.
China clay or pit props, perhaps a load of grain,
Railway lines or barrels, she hauled 'em just the same.

Later sold to Spaniards and then renamed *Maria*,
To roam the Bay of Biscay during her career.
She bunkered coal for liners, carried iron to France,
Dodging foe in wartime, taking then her chance.

She was not big or glamorous, but defied the odds,
Guided by her steering gear made of chain and rods.
Her end was very near, by scrap or fatal rust,
But luckily retrieved by an honest trust.

Now preserved in London, moored up in the docks,
Serving as a gallery for promotions and workshops,
A triumph for our heritage, especially maritime,
For she floats again as the *Robin* – and flies the red ensign.

THE SAGA OF THE *FLYING ENTERPRISE*, 1951

It was the *Flying Enterprise* steaming to the west;
Her master, Captain Carlson, was about to stand a test.
Christmas day in '51 he met a violent storm,
Standing out in history greater than the norm.
Days and weeks she hove to in heaving seas of green;
Tossing, wild and pitching, cracks on deck were seen.

In this mighty hurricane she rolled her beams close under,
And structural damage evident began to break asunder.
Four hundred miles past Land's End an SOS was sent
To save the crew and passengers now the ship was spent.
The troopship *General Greely* came upon the scene,
And the Yankee steamer *Southland*, nearby on the beam.

They could not launch the lifeboats – the list was too severe –
So jumped into the water as rescuers pulled near.
Ten passengers plus crew were saved, chilled through to the bone,
Leaving Captain Carlson aboard there, all alone.
Battered by the giant waves, to port she heeled and listed –
Included in her cargo was pig iron, which had shifted.

Forty-five degrees or more she lurched and there she stayed.
Failing then to right herself, on her side she laid.
A deep-sea tug, the *Turmoil*, eventually came by.
The mate of her, Ken Dancy, in a case of do-or-die,
Leapt aboard the stricken ship to give a helping hand,
Aiding Captain Carlson and his vessel far from land.

Those two men together in a Herculean task
Hauled a cable inboard and made the tug all fast.
Steadily they towed her, slowly, every day,
Till closing near to Falmouth, forty miles away,
The weather worsened once again, then the towline parted.
Ship's demise now obvious, our heroes, broken-hearted,
Walked along the funnel, as it was laying flat,
Made it to a lifeboat, and that, my friends, was that!

Two men well remembered for an epic of its day –
Maritime tradition and bravery held sway.
The sea's a haughty mistress and frequently takes charge,
Testing all our seamen and mariners at large.

STV *ROYSTON GRANGE*

Worse things happen at sea, they say – worse things happen at sea.
In '72 this came true with the tanker *Tien Chee*.
Within dense fog near the River Plate, she collided with a freighter.
Petrol gushed from shattered tanks, exploding seconds later.

The other ship, the *Royston Grange*, in fatal rendezvous,
Lost seventy-four razed on her – all passengers and crew.
Full cargo holds of butter ignited overall,
Fused in mighty fireball that left no chance at all.

Ten thousand tons of vessel went up in lethal blaze –
No time, then, for rescue or warning sound to raise.
Montevideo close at hand, bodies still entrapped,
The Houlder's ship towed away and later on just scrapped.

By the Tower of London, in All Hallows Church,
There is a stained-glass window – if carrying out research –
In commemoration colour with burning-red repands,
Depicting *Royston Grange* in memory of all hands.

Worse things happen at sea, they say,
Worse things happen at sea. . . .

THE SHIPPING FORECAST

From Faeroes and Forties to North German Bight,
Humber and Thames, Dover and Wight,
Plymouth and Portland, Biscay and Sole,
Fastnet and Lundy (where puffins patrol).

Iceland and Malin plus Cromarty,
Fair Isle, Fisher and South Irish Sea,
Trafalgar and Fitzroy, Forth and the Tyne,
Bailey, Rockall, Shannon in line.

Accepted by shore folk, but maybe obscure,
Though focal for seamen sailing offshore,
Diction is clear in a slow measured pace,
For writing it down in a nautical space.

Viking, Utsire, of course Hebrides,
These regions distinct as part of our seas,
Enduring and well known by seamen out there,
Remembering well the old Finisterre.

All form of vessels that steam round our land
Depend on the weather for voyages planned,
With ferries and freighters, fishermen too,
Tankers and coasters just butting through.

'Prospects are stormy, visibility low' –
Whatever the forecast it's handy to know.
Winds perhaps veering or pointer to fall,
A mariner's ready for sunshine or squall.

Goodnight, gentlemen, and good sailing.

THE SIX-O'CLOCK SWILL
(In Australia / New Zealand)

Remember the Down Under swill boys, when pubs were shut at six,
With only half a dogwatch to drink our daily fix.
We grafted all day to earn our pay – seamen in our prime –
'Twas 5 p.m. afore allowed to spend our social time.

With schooners of beer in excellent cheer we joined the other ABs
From various craft with motley crews arrived from overseas.
The Shaw Savill ships or Blue Star and tramps the likes of Hain's,
Among the vessels loading or discharging under cranes.

Ale was shot into glasses from a tap on the end of a hose,
Held in a crate and paid for straight – then thrust to under your nose.
Our favourite tipple went down well, swilling and drinking apace;
Too soon, to soon, eight bells were struck – we had too get out of the place.

"Carry out, carry out!" the cry went up, so we ordered the best on the coast;
With beer on our hip and away from the ship we followed a willing host.
We revelled then and had our fill – perhaps stayed there till morn,
Kissed the sheilas, bid farewell and back on board by dawn.

Another hard day, but on the way to repeat a fine night ashore,
Showered and shaved in no time – then straight for the bar-room door.
So if you recall the fifties and the six-o'clock swill, like me,
Do you remember Auckland and Ma Gleeson's by the quay?

THE STANDARD-BEARER

I am a standard-bearer; I'm striding mighty proud,
Conscious of my posture as I pass the cheering crowd.
My standard is a tribute – represents the men,
Who served and died for country, plus veterans since then.

You may see the likes of me, with gloves and belt so white,
Leading homage with my colleagues in uniforms alike.
Since the Romans with their *signum* or vexillum toting rag,
There has been a banner-bearer with his special flag.

An honour and a privilege, I do the job for free;
I ask no fame or kudos, nor princely sum or fee.
Unabashed to shed a tear at funerals where I go,
I'm thinking of my freedom and debt I surely owe.

I stand tall at the functions, or freedom of a city,
The cenotaphs, or marching where bands beat out a ditty,
'Tis fitting and my duty, while the last post sounds ahead,
For me to dip the standard, remembering the dead.

*Dedicated to all standard-bearers – inspired by "Wings" Barry,
MNA, Bristol Branch.*

THE STOKEHOLD

I passed a big ship steaming into a heavy sea,
Powered by steam engines – to some a mystery.
She had a 'woodbine' funnel, forcing up the draught,
So I knew the 'black gang' were working at their craft.

Trimmers kept fuel coming, with barrows full of coal,
Often from the 'tween decks an' the vessel on the roll.
Firemen fed the furnaces, making constant steam,
Choking and half roasted, eyes smarting to extreme.

Several of those ovens under their command,
In non-stop roar of engines and boiler's fierce demand.
Attired in vest and blue jeans, sweat rag duly clutched,
Leather belt worn backward or buckle seared when touched.

Iron doors hinged open, facing fervent heat,
An art to shovelling coal, trying to keep your feet,
Raking and a-poking to stop clogging of the bars,
Sweating bodies shining over tattoos and the scars.

An eye upon the gauges to keep things just precise,
Striving with their working tools – devil, rake and slice –
Used to sort the clinker out afore eight bells applied,
Trimmers hauled the ashes up and dumped 'em overside.

Well beneath the waterline these men earned their pay,
Supplying red-hot caverns – 200 tons a day.
I passed that big ship steaming many years ago,
Knowing that her 'black gang' were slaving down below.

THE TS *INDEFATIGABLE*

They travelled up from villages, the city and the fen,
Young lads sent to *Inde* to train as sailor men.
Most were only fourteen – raw or streetwise youth –
Some from broken families, all of them uncouth.

Arriving at this training ship upon the Menai Straits,
Embarking on a tough regime once passing through the gates,
Instilled in them a discipline, learning all the while,
Comradeship and fortitude to go that extra mile.

There was no mollycoddling while gaining self-respect,
Marching to a bugle band and drummers' beat erect,
Torn away from apron strings, standing quite assured,
Confident and able afore they went abroad.

Sitting on old Nozzer's Rock, they never will forget
Reflecting on the values they'll also not regret,
The vista of Mount Snowdon across the other shore,
While manning up the whalers and pulling on the oar.

Rodney, Drake, Raleigh, Hood were divisions there;
Leading hands and head boys served a handy share,
Supervised on navy lines by officers and peers,
The making of our seamen all throughout the years.

Developing a character, bringing to the fore
Reliant sturdy mariners in times of peace or war.
Eventually they sailed away – began a life at sea –
Joining ranks of hardy souls with *Inde* pedigree.

Many served as captains, others came ashore,
All of them indebted for biding there before,
Recalling all the standards and qualities back then
That set the course of youngsters and turned 'em into men.

*I was PO boy, No. 98 Hood Division, from January 1956 to July
1957.*

THE *TREGENNA*

Picture yourself in a convoy on a wild September day
Astern of a ship named *Tregenna* – just three cables away.
She's steaming along at eight knots with a cargo of steel in the hold,
Pitching heavy in head seas, into the spray and the cold.

When all of a sudden a U-boat, dodging the escort screen,
Fired a salvo of tin fish, tracking through fast . . . unseen.
This lethal spread of torpedoes became *Tregenna*'s death knell,
Just as her bow descended headlong into the swell.

It was a fatal plunge that the ship was in,
Breached below her deck line, through the plates so thin.
Her freight stowed heavy and low, beneath an empty space,
Quickly led to foundering when water took its place.

The ocean rushed in so quickly, leaving no time to prepare –
She dived on her nose and kept going, stern shot high in the air.
The watch on the bridge jumped clear, perchance or not to drown –
Only four abandoned her as the ship went down.

Now you have the story when in the vessel astern.
Two minutes it took to reach there, horrified to learn
There was no sign of *Tregenna* – just Atlantic waves,
Thirty-three men within her bound to deep-sea graves.

Sinkings were so frequent on a convoy's run,
But our merchant seamen still defied the Hun.
One reason why our monument stands there to remember
Is for the likes of these men who died here that September.

The Tregenna *sailed from Halifax in convoy HX71 on 5 September 1940. On 17 September the* U65 *fired the torpedoes that struck the* Tregenna *just as the ship pitched forward. She did not recover and stood vertically, briefly, before sinking. She was 413 feet long, carrying 8,500 tons of steel. This catastrophe was observed by men of the* Filleigh *who were in station less than two minutes' travelling time directly astern of* Tregenna. *According to the second mate, she had sunk in less than forty seconds.*

There were four survivors.

THE SS *TREVESSA*

'Twas in the Indian Ocean in 1923,
The *Trevessa* perished by the head in a raging sea.
Loaded in Port Pirie, her cargo heavy zinc,
Bound in time for Antwerp until about to sink.
The heaving seas were flooding in, the vessel taking water,
In the hold the concentrates like wet cement or mortar.
Pumps there could not handle it as bilges could not drain;
Engineers tried everything, but toiled and fought in vain.

Abandoning *Trevessa* in the early hours of morn,
Shocked by her quick foundering soon after in the storm,
Embarking in two lifeboats the crew of forty-four
Commenced upon their voyages of epic ocean lore.
The wooden craft were clinker-built, eight-foot beam and strong,
A single mast with lugsail and twenty-six feet long.
The mate in charge of one boat cast off to sail and row
Westward to Mauritius – 2,000 miles to go.

The old man took the other one to find Rodriguez Isle,
Mostly in good spirits in merchant-navy style.
They tried to sail together, but after six rough days
The mate's boat proved the slower so went their separate ways.
Keeping up the headway, they pulled at times with oars,
Ignoring painful sunburn and agonising sores.
They lived on basic rations, doled out with discipline,
Plus cigarettes with matches and baccy in a tin.

The seventeenth day in the old man's boat saw two men pass away;
Nine succumbed in the other one from exposure, cold and spray,
Though four of them delirious carried out self-slaughter
By ignoring well-known orders and drinking of salt water.
Captain Cecil Foster had braved the First World War,
Knew how to stock the lifeboats as he'd been sunk before,
Stowing extra water and tins of milk condensed.
Along with hard ship's biscuits carefully dispensed.

Experience and foresight served them very well –
He'd saved the lives of many with now a tale to tell
Of surviving heavy seas, trying to steer a course
Through extremes of weather and latitudes of horse.
Days then weeks were counted, declining all the while,
Till navigating coral reefs off Rodriguez Isle.
Mauritius-bound, the mate's crew later made landfall,
Carried then ashore – for they could not walk at all.

The zinc concentrates were loaded in the form of a kind of slime, which water could not percolate. The sounding rod could not detect water in the holds; nor could the bilge pumps reach it. Engineers started to cut off the heads of the rivets in the collision bulkhead to allow the water to escape into the forepeak, where the pumps could reach it. However, the bulkhead began to bulge and crack and they were forced to give up the attempt.

THE TUG CONTROLLER

The agent's on the golf course, the ships are steaming near;
I'm waiting to give out orders, but nothing's yet quite clear.
The *Gear Bulk* may be cancelled – we don't know if she'll go.
My lads are ready waiting and I really want to know.

The weather isn't clever, the forecast not so good;
A car boat now wants three tugs – but two I understood.
Now I've lost a deckhand – his motor wouldn't go.
And trouble with the lock gates – they are running slow.

There's one man phoned in sick, so I'm jumping up the line,
And another stuck in traffic who won't get there in time.
Then we have some pilots trying to change tugs round –
It's best if we don't let 'em, so we stand our ground.

The *Giant* must be shifted – just across the dock –
An' a tanker may be loading if she makes last lock.
It's not only this tide where things I have to nurse,
But I'm dealing with the next one, where things look bloody worse.

I'm trying to give out orders, but I'm foiled at every turn.
Another vessel sailing – she wants one on the stern.
There are ifs and buts and maybes all throughout the tide –
It's enough to drive one mad, but I take it in my stride.

I think I have it sorted and the programme worked out right.
Nothing now can go wrong – but then again, it might.
All is set – the die is cast – my dinner's on the table,
Then I get a phone call: the vis' is half a cable!

It's not so bad on weekdays I'm in the office chair;
It's Saturdays and Sundays I pull my greying hair.
And of course I do it, though my diction's fruity,
But how I love my weekends – *when I'm not on duty*.

THE TUG CONTROLLER'S PRAYER

Let the engines start on the tugs,
The crews be timely on board.
Make sure there's tea in their mugs
As the ships come in from abroad.

May the weather stay calm and clear,
And everyone's on the ball,
So when the vessels draw near
Nobody calls me at all!

THE UNKNOWN SEAMAN

Close by our city monument, along the old Welsh Back,
You will see a dedication on a double plaque
Fixed upon the wavy seats that represent the sea.
It's for the Unknown Seaman remembered on this quay.

He travelled over oceans, but never sought the fame –
A real but faceless mariner who did not leave his name,
For the waves will hold no headstones or mark upon the deep,
And for the Unknown Sailor no narrative to keep.

But here we'll keep a welcome for each and every one
Of those perhaps that slipped the net with details simply gone.
Rightly we encompass them, whether near or far,
Joining all our seamen now resting 'cross the bar.

THE VETERANS

Cheers to the men in blazers with their memories of old,
Proudly wearing badges and tributes of the bold.
They belong to different units from the forces or the sea;
They stood fast for their country and the likes of you and me.

You will sight them at the squares and the cenotaph parades,
And standing to attention by the British Legion graves.
You will see them selling tickets for the charities involved,
And travelling round in coaches for reunions in the cold.

You will see them in Toc H and the battlefields of France,
Or performing gentle two-steps at a military dance.
You will spot them socialising – propping up the bar.
In fact you'll spot them anywhere in places near and far.

They are a little older than when they served their time.
The ranks may be a little crooked when they march or stand in line.
Many are sprouting hair from their noses and the ears,
But also that's what happens when you're getting on in years.

You may see the standard-bearer showing off the colours
At the van of stalwarts – all his band of brothers.
Their pedigree is noted while standing ramrod-straight,
Boots and medals gleaming with a beret on the pate.

Some are grumpy granddads, but most have a welcome smile,
And all remember comrades that forged an extra mile.
So when you meet a veteran with a badge upon his cap,
Bid a fond good day to him – he may salute you back.

THE *VINDICATRIX*

Have you heard of Mrs Drysdale? No reason why you should,
Unless you were a *Vindi* boy recalling pretty good.
She's the smartly painted figurehead from your training ship,
Which started life in '93 down a launching slip.

Many thousand old boys have memories of her –
Men from *Vindicatrix* I'm sure will all concur,
Training there was tough, discipline a blast,
But the making of a seaman from boy to man at last.

They came, perhaps, from cities, a village or the plough,
And grew aboard the *Vindi* – with Drysdale on the bow –
Learning by the hard times, the hunger and the strife,
The hale-and-hearty culture and friends made there for life.

The lads were taught seafaring ways afore they went abroad,
Instilled in them the values that helped them stand assured.
Eventually they sailed away, each with doughty crew,
Plying trade around the world where the duster flew.

They joined the ranks of steadfast men who kept our commerce flowing,
Withstanding foe and stormy seas when the winds were blowing,
All for one and shipmates when the devil knocks,
Stemming from their early days hard by Sharpness Docks.

A kindred spirit bonds them, by sailing neath the stars,
The sea their life and laughter when living under spars.
Boldly, then, they stood the worst, in peace, or war convoys –
Nothing less would one expect from *Vindicatrix* boys.

THE VISIT

I'm an old shellback, pushing seventy-three,
Living in the Midlands far from the nearest sea.
The oceans that I sailed on seemed a long, long way to go,
Till I was paid a visit by younger brother Joe.

We drank some wine and whisky – all day we swung the lamp,
Talked of spells when young and bold, of coasters and the tramp,
The time we lost the lifeboats when going to Baltimore,
Fog and icebergs on the Banks, the marvellous things we saw.

The South American Saint Line down the River Plate,
Loading coal at Durban with a now dead drinking mate,
Recalling months on tankers up the Gulf to Aberdan –
The temperature was bloody hot an' we didn't have a fan.

Runs around the 'Medi' and the liner trips,
Torrid coasts round Africa, all those merchant ships,
The shifting of the cargo at Georgetown's river mouth,
Then sugar from Havana to Formosa in the south.

The 'maid in Copenhagen an' men that gave their all,
Ashore there in Cape Breton it's reversing waterfall,
Long voyage from Australia loaded down with grain,
Fighting off the elements and awesome hurricane.

We spoke of many ladies that came within our spell
(And the one that foxed us at the Prince of Wales Hotel),
All the bars around the world where we slaked our thirst,
Especially East of Suez, where the best is like the worst.

Hauling back those youthful years in nostalgia's wallow,
Destiny was then – not now I have old age to follow.
Made me feel alive again – brought back my life at sea,
Commending all the years we spent, hard but roaming free.

I dreamt I'd go to Hull again and find a ship to sail,
Wander down to Postengate, discharge book on the rail.
Alas, I woke to memories – it's impossible to go.
Just spellbound by that visit from my younger brother Joe!

205

THE WESTERN OCEAN

I'm a Western Ocean mariner and I'll tell you if I can
Of awesome winter weather encountered here by man.
The seas build up with fury over miles of storm-tossed waves;
Hulls of ships are pounded and steering misbehaves.

Clouds are tattered rags amid the frequent squall,
Merging with the streaking peaks many storeys tall.
The air it feels like buckshot in the form of spray;
Wind is banshee howling through rigging in the way.

A-hogging and a-sagging, we ride the raging main.
Fore and aft with shaking mast the vessel wracks with strain.
Rolling and a-pitching in vast and lengthy swells,
Thundering seas crashing down, filling up the wells.

We dare not run before it – we'd poop our stern asunder.
We must not run along it – we'd roll ourselves right under.
The motion of a corkscrew, she spirals up and round,
Crashing into head seas with a 'whoomping' sound.

Half a mile from crest to crest in rolling hills of brine,
Ship trembling now, but climbing – only just in time.
Arriving on a summit, we take a diving plunge,
Dropping down into a trough with stomach-churning lunge.

The stern would lift, engine race, the screw would clear the water,
Speeding in its freedom – vibrating through the quarter.
Shovelled up the hawsepipes, a green sea thumps the prow,
Shooting tons to leeward off the flooded bow.

Battened down and hove to, waiting out the weather,
Standing tricks and watches working there together,
A sturdy ship beneath me and doughty crew beside –
A Western Ocean seaman takes it in his stride.

THE YELLOW FLEET

Nasser closed the Suez Canal in the Six-Day War,
Trapping ships in Bitter Lakes for seven years or more,
Fourteen deep-sea vessels, dust-covered by the sand,
Came to be the 'Yellow Fleet' in wind blown off the land.

Different nationalities anchored close together,
Biding out their time in the desert weather.
The UK ships *Melimpus* with the *Scottish Star*,
Also *Invercargill* and *Agapenor* not far.

Norwegians water skiing, archery with Yanks,
Bulgarians and British, all officers and ranks,
Held their own regattas carefully organised;
The Polish and the Frenchmen also fraternised.

Crews of foreign seamen, including Swedes and Czechs,
Picked the teams for soccer – playing on the decks.
They swapped each other's goods and partied in the shade,
Even formed a post office where special stamps were made.

Finally in '75, two ships left the scene –
Münsterland and *Nordwind*, under their own steam,
Reached the port of Hamburg to waving and loud cheers,
The cargo worth a fortune after all those years.

Of the dozen others confined in their prime,
I'm clueless to their fate or outcome since that time.
It was not the life they chose, but was the life they got –
Yet another story of a seaman's diverse lot.

THEY BORE THE BRUNT

They sailed the seas to bear the brunt,
They steamed the courses laid,
Ten thousand miles their battlefront,
Unbacked and undismayed.

Fine seamen these of our great race,
From your seaport or town,
They risked their lives with danger faced
Until their ship went down.

Remember them – they held the line,
Won freedom on the way.
Remember them – their life was thine –
On Merchant Navy Day.

THEY DID NOT MAN THE BOMBERS

They did not man the bombers that rendered cities dead,
Or Hurricanes and Spitfires in dogfights overhead,
Nor fight the war as infantry pushing at the front,
Or as marine commandos or paratroops that jump.

They did not form in ranks, divisions or platoons,
Or march along to 'eyes right' with regimental tunes.
Civilian crews of seamen sailed to do their bit
On coastal runs or convoys until their ship was hit.

A kitbag on the shoulder after travelling on the bus,
They stepped aboard a gangway with the minimum of fuss.
There was little recognition for men that risked their lives,
But heroes just the same as in trenches or the skies.

They sailed away on oceans with a puny little gun
To face the lethal U-boats sent out by the Hun.
They brought the cargoes home, then returned for more,
Flying our red ensign all throughout the war.

TOMBO MARY'S

Apapa was the venue for our lads' run ashore,
On the coast of Africa where tourists never tour.
The bar was Tombo Mary's, where she ruled the roost all day;
Customers were seafarers – keen to spend their pay.

In this one-roomed shanty, with hard mud for a floor
(Palm fronds on the thatched roof and canvas for a door),
Our black mama, Mary – a wondrous female sight –
Would choose a handy sailor for her carnal joys at night.

Raised up on a dais just behind the bar
(The centre of attention from here to Calabar)
Was a huge four-poster bed with linen and fine lace,
Imported from some far-off land and taking pride of place.

It's where Mary held her lover boy for a torrid night of fun.
Piccaninnies and the bar staff, at the setting of the sun,
Would sleep below this raft of love, with tassels hanging red,
While the sailor did his duty in Tombo Mary's bed.

TORPEDOED

Torpedoed ships now lie in peace
Fathoms deep below,
Their crews now free from misery
Of convoy's evil foe.

A grey dawn over ocean graves
Swathe their history.
We remember, even so,
Blue roads to victory.

Many seamen gave their lives
So many miles away
For freedom we recall
On this Remembrance Day.

TRAWLERMEN

I'd like to speak of trawlermen that search the cruel seas,
Hunting for the fishes that dart off where they please,
To shoot the nets and haul 'em in, toiling day and night,
Risking limbs and humour in oceans breaking white.

Skipper in the wheelhouse unshaven in his chair,
Wedged in with his coffee and chatting on the air,
Tending to his mission and watching out for ships;
Gulls are wheeling all about, squabbling for the bits.

Wet and water everywhere, faces chapped and red,
Rolling and a-pitching with spraying overhead;
Little change of clothing and soaking all the time,
Living in their oilskins amid the salty grime.

The gutting of the cargo and chipping of the ice,
Lacking sleep, uncomfortable, no lubber's paradise,
Yearning for a dry bunk and warming bit of supper,
While freezing in the wind or rolling in the scupper.

Loud and noisy engines, pervading oily smell,
Dining on the 'prime' they caught, every day as well,
Snagging of the gear then mending is a chore –
Still our island fishermen return again for more.

Whether in the Arctic or another scene,
Maybe out of Brixham, Hull or Aberdeen,
In wind and snow they sally forth into frequent squalls,
Accepting all conditions, shooting out the trawls.

The nature of the job means uncertain pay,
Depending on the 'fixer' and prices on the day.
A good catch shows a bonus when hauling safe and sound,
Thinking of a pint or two now they're homeward-bound.

Hardy crews venture out to areas so vast,
Flying our red ensign whipping from the mast.
When you buy a bit of fish, wherever it is sold,
Spare a thought for trawlermen working in the cold.

SS *TREVESSA*'S ENSIGN

There was a young apprentice among *Trevessa*'s crew,
He carried off the duster from where the ensign flew,
For when his ship was sinking he abandoned with the rest,
And wore it in the lifeboat clutched around his chest.

It was a proud convention to fly it from the mast;
Now it helped preserve him until ashore at last.
His name was Arthur Phillips – he came from Barry town –
Brave to save the colours before his ship went down.

Not only is it bunting signalled from the yard,
But the emblem of our seamen held in high regard,
Round the world exalted through the shot and shell –
That's why it went with Arthur in his boat as well.

WE COULD MAN A BATTLESHIP
(The Merchant Navy Association.)

We could man a battleship, we could sail a scow –
Association members have not forgotten how.
We still remember Morse code and streaming of the log,
How to sail the wide world and navigate in fog.

We can wield a trusty sextant and box the compass round,
Pull a heavy piston to a chain block's rattle sound.
We could feed all hands, with plenty left for suppers,
Though the vessel's pitching and rolling to the scuppers.

We could anchor anywhere and count the shackles home,
Cleaning up, outward-bound, use the holystone,
Rig a stage or bosun's chair, throw a heaving line –
Most things being nautical we can do just fine.

We bade farewell to splicing and seamen's work by hand,
The cranky coal fired engine and steam-emitting gland,
But one thing may be lacking in these modern days
Is how to work the satnav or push-the-button ways.

So we sit back in retirement and think of olden times,
Like sweating in the tropics supping juice of limes.
Perhaps a Russian convoy freezing half to death,
As well as mighty hurricanes that take away one's breath.

Still, we know it's over as we contemplate a glass –
Nothing like a full life to make regrets so sparse.
We are baffled by technology and systems that are new,
This ever ready bunch of ours – this out-of-date old crew.

WE REMEMBER

As I wait beneath the trees,
Softly kissed by gentle breeze,
Pigeons, gulls and swans abound,
While our veterans gather round

By water's edge – just sublime –
Then recalling fraught wartime,
Assembled here for all to see,
For those that fought at Normandy.

Lucky us this summer's day,
We do remember – let us pray.

At the Merchant Navy Association Monument, 6 June.

WE MADE IT, KID

It was the world's worst journey across the Barents Sea
In a scattered Russian convoy, named PQ1 and 3,
Off the coast of Norway and round its Northern Cape,
Braving hidden U-boats and the Junkers 88.

A torpedo struck the hold, bearing tons of coiled barbed wire
Over aviation spirit – which exploded into fire.
Ordered to our stations, primed to abandon ship,
Struggling, taking crew off – the fire had forged a grip.

One man emerged from through it – he was all aflame,
Jacket, face, ears and hair; I didn't know his name.
His feet and hands were tattered as he fought to save his neck,
Over red-hot cargo that had blown up to the deck.

We pitched him in the lifeboat, where we beat him out,
Then cast off from our vessel as there was no doubt
The ship was doomed and sinking, rolling on her side,
Since another tin fish took its mortal ride.

Four days then we spent adrift in appalling weather,
This winter in the Arctic freezing all together.
The man just sat upon a thwart in ghastly awful pain,
Sheer open to the elements, but never did complain.

He may have been Canadian or perhaps a Yank
(It's difficult to have a chat with a gale upon your flank),
But he helped to pull along by leaning on his arms.
His hands had swollen treble – he couldn't use his palms.

The only thing he asked for, in those horrendous days afloat,
Was "Can you hold a fag for me, if I burn a smoke?"
Then came at dusk a rescue by a Russian fishing smack,
Who hauled us to a shelter in Murmansk's cul-de-sac.

He looked at me through frozen eyes; most of him was rigid,
But he cracked his face and from his mouth I heard "We made it, kid."
Next day in the refuge I was summoned to his bed,
Where this courageous seaman was lying there quite dead.

I do not know the history of this man I hardly knew,
For he was picked up previously from another crew.
Years later on, enquiring – his name may be O'Brien,
But I'll not forget such dignity and his courage of a lion.

On 30 March 1942, the SS Induna *(part of convoy PQ13, which was scattered by severe storms) was sunk by two torpedoes from the U376. The SS* Induna *had previously picked up men from the whale ship* Silja *and the SS* Ballot. *The doomed seaman is believed to have been off the SS* Ballot, *which had sailed from New York under the Panamanian flag and joined the convoy from Iceland. She was then attacked by dive-bombers and lost steam. Sixteen men were transferred to the SS* Induna.

The above story is from a report by a crew member of the SS Induna *who survived the war. There is a grave in Murmansk with the name O'Brien, but no ship is mentioned. Ironically both the* Silja *and the* Ballot *– though casualties – eventually made it to Murmansk.*

WHEN

When you want to roam the world and leave the apron strings at home,
When you'd like to drop your girl and leave the booze alone,
When you're facing storms aplenty and need to make a lee,
Well, my son, just think of going to sea.

When you're in a dead-end job and you need another line,
When you're going nowhere fast and wasting precious time,
When you're feeling low and desperate to be free,
Then, my lad, I'd wander off to sea.

When you're getting in the way and maybe tired of life,
When progress is on hold and you're putting up with strife,
When you're in the mood to take a tip from me,
Then, my son, you should go to sea.

When you need to feel fresh air and build your self-esteem,
When you want to be a cog in a total different team,
When you feel the wanderlust, I think that you'll agree –
Well, young man, it's time to go to sea.

When you're like a lighthouse in the desert (bright, but of no use),
When all you have is enemies and want to call a truce,
When you turn a deaf one to your elders and buck a guilty plea,
Please, my boy, why don't you go to sea?

When you're winding up your dad and upsetting poor old Mother,
When you're teasing little sister and fighting elder brother,
When you're nothing but a pain and always on a spree,
Well, my lad, please listen, and run away to sea!

WHITE BERETS

They wear the berets of white, my friends, they wear berets of white,
For they sailed on Russian convoys, wondering day and night
If they'd reach their destination in Murmansk, further north,
Chancing Hitler's bombers or submarines sent forth.

Hauling vital cargoes, men were sorely tried,
Carrying on regardless though many went and died.
Seventy-eight the convoys that counted up the cost;
As there and back they lumbered, many ships were lost.

The wind would howl and shriek round ice upon the yard;
In fog, snow and violent storms, life was pretty hard,
Plodding on laboriously, guarding round the clock,
Sleepless nights and piping cold until they reached the dock.

They risked their lives steadfastly in dreadful bitter climes
Long ago, but veterans recall those vivid times.
That's why, my friends, I mention it, for they have earned the right
To proudly wear a beret in the shade of Arctic white.

LEST WE FORGET

There are no flowers on a sailor's tomb,
No welcome home from Flat Holm's loom.
Remember those in Neptune's deep,
On granite symbol for souls asleep.

Hailed in monument on Welsh Back,
Under trees by a harbour track,
To our valiant dead this tribute stands –
Atop the mast their ensign fans.

In becalmed and safe repose,
Revere this rock on a compass rose.
Let our mariners find a lee –
Lest we forget – on a Bristol quay.

MN BOOK OF REMEMBRANCE

You are cordially invited to pen a fitting word –
A tribute to a loved one, a mariner that served
In the merchant navy in peace or time of strife,
Thus record his memory and compliment his life.

Go read about a seafarer who died in time gone by,
Written down forever in a tome that does not lie.
His colleagues and his shipmates will be added to the roll,
Labelled there intently in copperplated scroll.

Alas, if carved in marble, a wall would be too wide
To mention all our mariners that went to sea and died.
Accept these pages sheltered and free from icy blast,
Clear to see by visitors and shellbacks from the past.

Not far from our monument on Bristol's cobbled quay
Are these named reluctant heroes who gave their lives at sea,
Contained within a special book inscribed by Princess Anne,
Cared for by St Stephen's Church – peruse it when you can.

THE GRUDGE FIGHT

There was no such thing as boredom aboard our training ship.
With officers abounding to give an ear a clip,
We couldn't get away with much with discipline so tight,
Once an altercation became a full-fledged fight.

Put to work one day, on a tank which must be filled –
A job involving water which accidentally spilled –
Myself and Terry Beagley set about each other.
A brawl took place so naturally while thumping one another.

Alas, our scrap was spotted by an officer on call,
Resulting in a grudge fight shortly watched by all.
The time was set for later – after evening stew;
Boxing gloves were found and seconds called up too.

The venue was an old barn set up as a gym;
Distempered walls were white around the boxing ring.
One hundred boys or more waiting there so keen –
Me and my old rival told to make it clean.

He wore blue for Raleigh – the house for which he stood.
My sash was all yellow – fighting for old Hood.
An officer of seamanship was the referee;
He was known as Beaky – John Firth to you and me.

Our local rule for grudge fights – to decide the one to win –
Was three minutes to a round until a towel's thrown in.
We touched our gloves to shake hands, then commenced to fight,
Continuing our differences that dark November night.

We both developed nosebleeds we couldn't stop at all,
So blood was spattered everywhere, including round the wall.
Both of us were fifteen – fit and stubborn boys –
Still there was no winner as we fought amid the noise.

On and on we battled till we could fight no more;
Raising up an arm each, the referee called a draw.
Our arguments were settled, friction at an end,
Our respect was mutual and Terry now my friend.

This fight took place in 1956 while aboard the training ship Indefatigable. *It was talked about for a long time. Terry Beagley became petty officer boy in charge of Raleigh Division, and I became petty officer boy in charge of Hood division.*

We met up again fifty years later and remained friends until his untimely death in 2010.

THE *MEDWAY QUEEN*

She is the *Medway Queen*, popular and fast,
With a jaunty rake of funnel and bunting from the mast,
The waving of the passengers leaning on the rail,
And jingle of the telegraph when about to sail.

Weathered canvas dodgers and lifebelts red and white,
Ensign flying proudly on halyard whipping tight,
Paddles swooshing easily, foaming as they churn,
Leaving wake ruler-straight trailing there astern.

Captain's orders from the bridge open to the weather,
Fascinating engines steaming hell for leather,
Called upon in wartime years for most valiant work,
She became the *Heroine* active at Dunkirk.

Seven thousand men she saved in terrifying times
When diverted from her war task of sweeping up the mines,
Earning crew awards for staving off the dread
And shooting down the enemy flying overhead.

Triple were her furnaces – Scotch boiler down below –
When built upon the Clyde ninety years ago.
She changed from burning coal, back in '38,
Using now red diesel to push along her freight.

Fifteen knots her best speed steaming there and back,
From Chatham down to Clacton, then a homeward tack.
To the wooden piers she'd regularly deliver,
On the estuary of the Thames and the Medway river.

That was long ago, of course, but after some review
The *Medway Queen* returned to us by ambition of a few,
Our merchant-navy heritage held by us so dear,
Restored to sea a fine ship to sail again this year.

A PRIVATE'S VIEW

Oh, bring us home from war, General – from the sunset red.
Return us to our families, friends and comfy bed.
We are finished with the Taliban, insurgents and the sand,
And need the sight of greenery on England's pleasant land.

Attempts to change this country is a dirty rotten joke,
For the enemy's enmeshed with common Afghan folk.
However just the cause, or how our fight explained,
Very much is lost – nothing worth is gained.

Try and fly me out of it with other weary troops;
Let me walk free streets again and change these desert boots.
I'll bet there is no end to it – a waste of life and time.
You see those yonder body bags? – They were friends of mine.

WESTON PIER

Come on, friendly tide, and wash away
The blackened embers from the day
When Weston Pier sent to the sky,
Shooting flames and smoke on high.

Mangled wreckage now remains
In bent and twisted metal frames,
All ashes left of seaside leisure
Upon our pier used for pleasure.

Still and all, there's lots to see –
Donkey rides and B & B,
Castles in the sand to build;
Chips are hot and cider chilled.

May local jokes abound,
Especially one going round –
Twinning towns on greeting card:
Burnham's on there; so is Chard.

Later on we'll have once more,
Better than the days of yore,
A landmark fitting seaside fame
At Weston-super-Mare again.

After the pier burnt down, 2008.

AIRPORT SECURITY

I often nip abroad to my little Spanish pad;
But oh, what drives me crazy and verging on the mad
Is striving through the airport via brash security
With boarding pass kept handy and passport for ID.

I'm told to take my coat off and stick it in a tray,
Plus wallet and my glasses (now cannot see my way),
Then my belt and loose change, watch and bunch of keys –
Continue on with trousers hanging round my knees.

Bossy sentries beckon, with a hounding look,
Through the body scanner – but still not off the hook.
I have to take my shoes off – what the devil for?
Then I'm shuffled forward across the scruffy floor.

Standing like a scarecrow, they start and frisk my arms;
When they reach my legs – well, that sets off alarms
For I'm not smuggling dynamite or toxic mad disease;
It's just a bit of metal in two replacement knees.

Finally I get through to find divested gear,
Looking for my laptop abandoned somewhere near;
Emerging in the duty-free, on towards the gate,
Overpriced the sandwiches while settling down to wait.

Coming home through Malaga, security's a breeze –
Efficiently they nod me on, simply and at ease.
Easy Jet transports me back to Bristol's turf,
Then the maze of barriers while treated like a serf.

Oh, the joys of travelling to and from our land
Just to have a bit of fun by the sea and sand!
I suppose we must put up with it and endure the fuss
Or go perhaps the long way and catch a ruddy bus!

AN ENGLISH WEDDING

We are gathered here today, they say,
All waiting for the wedding;
Clean white shirts and ironed skirts,
Up the aisle we're heading.

Nervous groom making room,
Best man stood there blowing.
The bride is here, never fear,
All in white and glowing.

Something new, something blue
And a hidden garter;
He looks cute in a sombre suit,
Never looking smarter.

The oaths are said as the vicar read,
Rings slipped on the fingers;
No more a miss, she takes a kiss
From the groom – who lingers.

Down the aisle with a brilliant smile
The parents are just beaming,
Strolling out, all about,
Through the church door streaming.

Now stood mute for a photo shoot,
Confetti showered over,
Holding pose with a big red rose,
Our bride and Casanova.

The same holds sway in every way
For many young folks' marriage.
They look swell – we wish them well –
Sent off in a horse-drawn carriage.

BADMINTON

There's a brilliant game called badminton – I recommend you play.
It keeps you fit and healthy any given day.
You try to hit a shuttlecock with racquet very light –
It may be placed quite gently or smashed with all your might.

The fun part is the rally, plus gaining of the points,
Trying to foil opponents and their creaking joints.
There is cursing, there is laughter in this wicked game –
Fantastic shots are possible, but no two hits the same.

Frustration takes its toll when returns are easy lost,
Or contact with the net to you and partner's cost;
Perhaps an awful judgement leaving a line call,
Then finding to bewilderment it wasn't out at all.

A jump smash is the fastest at many miles an hour,
A drop shot gently placed or forehand sent with power;
A block shot and a push shot, backhanders too, of course,
Are sometimes thrust with poise or deceptive force.

The ladies and the gentlemen team up to whack the 'bird',
Performing acrobatics bordering on absurd.
It never is intentional to miss the thing in flight –
But oh, the satisfaction if you return it right!

Skills are varied wildly by players at the time –
Some of them, like me, a little past their prime.
But the best and worst of them, as evident by score,
Have one thing in common – they all return for more.

BLOODY SAND BAY

All bloody clouds, not bloody funny,
All bloody rain and never sunny.
No bloody flowers, no bloody grass,
All bloody sand up to your arse,
In Sand Bay.

The bloody wind, the bloody gales,
Bloody washing blown out like sails.
No bloody buses, no bloody shops,
That bloody pong it's on the crops,
In Sand Bay.

Bloody dustmen they're bloody late,
Bloody rubbish left by the gate.
Bloody postman – 'snot bloody right!
Don't get the bloody mail till night,
In Sand Bay.

Bloody tourists, bloody Brummies,
Bloody kids without their mummies.
Bloody noisy and in the way,
Never bloody understand a word they say,
In Sand Bay.

Bloody pub too bloody near,
And bloody booze is bloody dear.
Bloody open till very late,
Bloody rolling home in drunken state,
In Sand Bay.

Bloody smoking costs me dearly,
But, like Sand Bay, I like it really.
The bloody weed, I'm bloody trying
To give it up; my nerves are crying,
In Sand Bay.

That's why my hamlet is taking stick,
Cos of the habit I'm trying to kick.
Bloody moaning is my way,
So take no notice of what I say,
In Sand Bay.

But I'm telling you the gauntlet's thrown –
I'm existing in a smokeless zone.
It's bloody hell in Sand Bay.

BAND OF BROTHERS: D-DAY

We sailed from old England across the blue sea,
Gaining the beach at French Normandy.
In a dip in the soil I looked around,
Seeing our Fred smacked to the ground.
Then I spied Harry, bloodied and still,
Alongside a mate – alas, it's poor Bill.

Shouting us on, our tough Sergeant Bruce,
With holes in his helmet and arm hanging loose.
Onward and upward, we tried to gain cover,
Hearing young men beseeching their mother.
There were blinded and limbless spread on the sand,
Some calling for medics to give 'em a hand.

Loaded with backpacks the going was tough –
Shooting and running, we made for the bluff.
Soon I found Tommy shot through the neck –
The havoc and carnage continued on yet,
My colleagues, my friends, comrades-in-arms,
Dropping like flies with guns in their palms.

Too many men I had known for so long
Lay wounded or dead or simply just gone.
We fought on the grounds – in from the sea –
For freedom, for God, for whole victory.
I do so remember – will never forget –
My band of brothers lying there yet.

From a shipmate who was there.

BLOSSOM HILL

I wanted somewhere special for Chris and me in Spain –
I reckoned not too far away, just an hour or two by plane.
We searched in Andalucia and found a *casa* fit the bill.
We loved it, so we bought it; its name is Blossom Hill.

Nearby is Mount Maroma and the sun comes up behind,
Warming up our balcony where frequently we dined.
Later in the swimming pool we splash about at will,
And we are going to plant a lemon tree soon at Blossom Hill.

My favourite bougainvillea has fantastic flowers of red;
Every day the eagles soar majestic overhead.
There is a praying mantis that likes our window sill,
And occasionally a lizard visits Blossom Hill.

Egrets wading peacefully, nothing to disturb;
Rustling in the pepper trees giving shade superb.
Wine is cheap and plentiful – we often have our fill
Lazing in the sunshine there at Blossom Hill.

It's nice to have some family out to stroll along the beach,
Or take em up some mountain track beyond the tourists' reach,
Cruising on the boat trips where dolphins play and thrill,
Then later watch the shooting stars over Blossom Hill.

A *cabrero* takes his sheep out, with his goats as well,
A 'tingling' and a 'bongling' sounding from each bell.
We sit and learn our Spanish – worries almost nil,
Until recalled to England away from Blossom Hill.

Lake Vinuela, October 2008

CRICKET

When I was a young lad and given a bat,
The first ruddy ball I gave it a whack;
And so I was hooked on our great British game
A long time ago, but I still feel the same.

The great Denis Compton with brilliance and flair,
Len Hutton performing with caution and care,
Don Bradman another – in green baggy cap –
These were my heroes I'd copy and clap.

Playing the game in all kinds of weather,
Embracing the sound of willow on leather,
Facing the pacemen I'd give it a go,
Aiming for boundaries – six in a row.

Nicking a fast one, avoiding the slips,
Sweeping a wide ball by turning my hips,
I'd steer such a beauty over silly mid-on,
Tapping and gardening when the over is gone.

On matches for county and overseas tours,
I'd swipe the pace bowlers for sixes and fours,
Then striking and placing to deep extra cover,
Running again and adding another.

Ignoring the sledging by slogging a flipper,
Seeing despair on the face of their skipper,
Discounting appeals and shouts of "Howzat?"
I finished my game and carried my bat.

Then when I'm bowling I use my right arm,
Yorkers and beamers causing alarm,
Expecting a teammate to catch a ball clean,
Or keeper to stump when prospects are seen.

Sending a 'Bunsen', confusing the foe,
Urging the Judges to tell 'em to go.
Leg before wicket, no use to linger –
The umpiring chap has pointed his finger.

I've played at the Oval and Gabba as well,
Old Trafford and Sydney – I expect you can tell.
All is a lie and not quite what it seems,
Though I live for my cricket – it was all in my dreams!

CHARLIE

I could have called him Sabre, Rex or maybe King –
He was a German shepherd – a regal name for him.
But no, I called him Charlie; he answered to his call,
Big and black and beautiful, the proudest dog of all.

He guarded home and family till I came home from sea;
Devoted and so loyal, he nuzzled up to me.
Later on, in old age, his hips would give him pain,
Then taking of his tablets he'd up and run again.

Eventually they wouldn't work – he flaked out on the lawn.
All night I kept him company, the pair of us forlorn.
It hurt too much to move him – we knew the end was nigh;
His love and comprehension looked me in the eye.

My pal, my friend, my trusted hound, I had to let you go,
That well-remembered day in May so long ago.
Nothing here on earth could make my sorrows drown
That day I paid a local vet to put old Charlie down.

CONCORDE

Concorde, Concorde, Bristol's bird,
Her sonic boom no longer heard.
A pity though and sad for us –
Next best thing is a flying bus.

We marvelled at our speedy dart,
Assembled here in state of art,
Engines thrusting just sublime,
Scudding high before her time.

Born with dreams this super ride,
Built with vision, flown with pride,
Far too young to be too old,
Shelved at peak not to be sold.

Many fans are saddened now
Since our beauty took a bow.
We will remember – won't forget –
Our graceful, wondrous, world's best jet.

November 2003

DIAMOND JUBILEE
(Thames Diamond Jubilee Pageant, 3 June 2012)

For sixty long years we have been ruled by our queen –
A wonderful lady, brave and serene.
A waterborne pageant to show our thanks
Was held on the river with crowds on the banks.

A thousand or more under way at the start,
Pulling and paddling and proud to take part.
Foreshore hurrahs were often let rip
To fabulous craft on the seven-mile trip.

Bunting abundant, white, red and blue,
Ringing of church bells sounding out too,
Splendid the barge our queen was aboard,
On par with others so fondly restored.

To add to her jewels in the shape of tears,
A jubilee diamond to go with the cheers,
Firework displays, street parties galore –
Her subjects now wish her many years more.

DON'T CRY FOR ME

Don't cry for me when I'm gone –
I've done my time, I've sung my song,
Smoked the rolls, drunk the wine,
Self-inflicted, the fault is mine.

No regrets, I've been content;
I'll guess you'll know which way I went,
So, my loved ones near and far,
Let me go across the bar.

For the wheel has rolled, it's my turn now,
Happy in old age to take a bow.
I've drifted off to catch the tide –
One day I'll greet you on the other side.

FLYING TO INDIA

I'm on a train – it's clacking away,
Bearing me on holiday.
Let the railway take the strain
On the way to an aeroplane.
At the airport checking in,
Get rid of case and all within,
Ambling round the duty-free,
Buying goods that's right for me,
Crossword done with favourite pen,
Waiting to board a DC10.
Watching screens for boarding gate,
The plane is there – not too late.
One by one we climb aboard,
Eager now for flight abroad,
Hurtling along at take-off speed,
Expect a drink the travellers need,
Soaring away and into the air,
Leaving behind the troubles and care,
Settling down for a nine-hour flight
Among the stars in the night,
Stewardess with cheery grin
Serving me a double gin,
Digging in to airline tucker –
Not much there, wait till supper –
TV movie, another brandy,
Booze allowance comes in handy.
Walk about to ease the cramps,
Dozing when they dim the lamps.
Landing now as day is dawning,
Advance the clocks – all are yawning.

Clear their customs to Goa's soil,
Shed some clothes and begin to boil –
The weather now is really hot,
Not all cold like England's got.
Climb upon a rickety bus –
Little room for all of us.
Safely there in hotel's cool,
Shortly then in the swimming pool.
A long old journey, but holy cow,
Can't you see I'm happy now!

December 2010

OK, it wasn't a DC 10 and it wasn't on time, etc., but this was scribbled using my imagination while on the train from Reading to Gatwick.

EVERY MAN SHOULD HAVE A SON

Every man should have a son to carry on the line –
A father would be lucky if he had a son like mine.
He did not want to go to sea – like his dear old dad.
Fair enough, he went his way – I could not blame the lad.

He is a chip off my old block, so I love him (not too much).
Perhaps I haven't shown it – sometimes lacked a touch –
But proud of him I've always been; I did the best I could.
Surely over all the years he grew and understood.

My boy dealt with troubles throughout his youthful ride,
Triumphs and disasters taken in his stride.
I could boast for ages of the virtues of my son;
The vices I won't mention – nor sins he did for fun.

"Less is more," a wise man said, so I'll finish this quite soon.
Suffice to say when Steve walks in he brightens up the room.

July 2012

HE'S BURIED BY THE GREENHOUSE

He's buried by the greenhouse – on his grave are flowers.
A family pet was Charlie – the memories are ours.
No more lead hanging down by the kitchen door,
Or metal bowl of water waiting on the floor.

No more friendly greeting, wagging of the tail,
Or barking at the postman delivering the mail.
No more grinding jaw, gnawing bones of pork,
Or spinning in delight at mention of a walk.

No more resting nose gently on my knee,
Or limpid shining eyes gazing up at me.
No more pleasant games, playing with a ball,
Or bounding back towards us, answering his call.

No more wet and smelly after being in the rain,
Or the look of triumph when he chased the cat again.
No more country strolls, sniffing round for hours –
He's buried by the greenhouse now, underneath the flowers.

GOA

When you walk the streets of Goa in this warm and pleasant land
You must treat the tracks with caution – take life in your hands,
For there are no proper pavements or straightened line of trees,
Just mostly reddish mud and cows roam where they please.

The traffic is just crazy with little rule of road
From the three-wheeled autorickshaws and the lorries' dodgy load
To taxis and the omnibus and pigs that shoot across,
The families on one scooter adding mayhem to chaos.

Women dressed in saris of brightly coloured thread,
Strolling very upright with load upon their head,
The labourer in a palm grove leaning on the spade,
Vendors of the sugar cane sitting in the shade.

Aromas come from cafés of fish and curried rice
All mixed in with torrid heat and smell of local spice,
Not-so-far-off beaches with sand like golden flour,
The pastel shades of sunset in the darkening hour.

The drunks that took the 'fenny' lying by the ditch
Surrounded by mosquitoes vying for a pitch.
Hippies are no trouble – just living on the cheap –
Backpackers an' all with trainers on the feet.

Travelling round the country, the buildings must be seen,
Waterfalls and rice paddies in marvellous shades of green,
The port of Marmagoa at the river's mouth
And the single track of railway line running north and south.

The little kids act wistful and wheedle for buckshees;
Sanitation non-existent – go behind the trees.
No one's in a hurry – it's laid-back Goan time –
Waiting very thirsty for a soda topped with lime.

Lots of goods awaiting in exotic marketplaces,
Assisted by the traders with cheerful smiling faces.
They will be very friendly and put you at your ease
And give a 'special price' to part you from rupees.

The sun is very kind, at our winter time of year;
Not so the Kingfisher – it's bloody awful beer.
So when you come to India and leave the cold behind,
I think you'll love old Goa – just keep an open mind.

2002

IT'S NOT FAR TO THE MOUNTAINS

It's not far to the mountains if distance made by crow,
Or the winding of the valley road snaking there below.
I'm lazing on our balcony looking to the east,
Soaking up the Spanish sun – troubled not the least.

An ideal spot for shellbacks recalling of the past,
Of life and love and glory days, most before the mast.
We sailed with our compatriots and harkened to the wise,
With convoy-hardened veterans whose brothers lost their lives.

Youth, they say, is wasted upon the thrusting young;
I reckon not and no regrets while on the lower rung.
We romanced girls wherever, from Cuba to Japan,
Then bade farewell forever – goodbye, Fairy Anne.

I grin and drink my coffee with a touch of brandy brew,
This long-toothed pensioned seaman gazing at the view.
The goats and sheep go 'bongling' past for their daily graze,
Reflections intermittent as I meet their ovine gaze.

So here in Andalucia, where the eagles soar,
A far cry from my tramping days and the breaker's roar,
I'm thankful for the memories and happy to review,
Till I take a cooling shower then light the barbecue.

IT'S WINTER NOW IN PORTISHEAD

It's winter now in Portishead
And gentle breezes blow
Seventy miles an hour
At twenty-five below.

Oh, how I love my Portishead
With snow up to my butt!
You take a breath of winter
And your nose gets frozen shut.

Yes, the weather here is wonderful,
So I guess I'll hang around.
I could never leave, you know,
Cos I'm frozen to the ground!

LOW EBB

"About twelve months," the doctor said.
"In one year's time you will be dead."
The brutal truth was thus revealed –
My lifetime partner's fate was sealed.

The cancer has a certain hold –
Too late now it was not foretold.
This deadly crab had within its grip
A dreadful vision of the fatal trip.

As I implored to the skies above,
"I beg of You, please, save my love,"
But now began that awful terror:
The fact has dawned – there is no error.

So it was the nightmare labour –
Each day now was one to savour.
My darling was so brave and bold,
The poignant hand of mine to hold.

What use now my puny strength?
We could only talk and muse at length.
Onward went the dwindling days,
The evil bent on its withering ways.

Unyielding pressure did something to me,
Blanked my brain, I ceased to be –
A rational being that was afraid,
Into a shell where panic raged.

Mind in turmoil, dreams of death –
Shall I join you, stop my breath?
No – others need me, I should not falter,
Must don a mask and refuse to alter.

Christmas came – New Year went,
The black disease went on hell-bent,
Then came the day through want of trying,
Lay my loved one surely dying.

Upon the pillow – goodbyes said –
Was laid to rest her peaceful head.
"Life goes on" is what they say;
Give me time . . . I'll find a way.

MRS AMY JONES ON HER WEDDING DAY

I have seen the Southern Cross hanging in the sky,
Scuba-dived on coral reefs, watching sharks go by,
Seen the dolphins somersault, and flying fish at play,
But none could match the beauty of Amy here today.

I have walked the pathways of a bluebell-sprinkled wood,
Watched the flight of kingfishers close to where I stood,
Observed the foreign sunsets and dimming of the light,
But nothing quite the image as Amy wearing white.

I have witnessed turtles hatched upon the beach,
Heard the fire and brimstone that teachers often preach,
Travelled over continents and covered many miles,
But I would shun 'em all for one of Amy's smiles.

I surveyed the snow on Fuji, and mountains on the way,
Visions of a mirage out across the bay.
Amy is a picture, but reminds me of another –
Credit where it's due – it's Heather, Amy's mother!

2 July 2016

MY FAVOURITE THINGS

Pictures of convoys in Arctic conditions,
Hearing the last post and bugle renditions,
The anchor engraved on one of my rings –
These are a few of my favourite things.

Paintings by children that turn out like doodles,
Teaching them how with drawings of poodles,
'Wine Drinker Me' that Dean Martin sings –
These are a few of my favourite things.

Brilliant ideas that come on in flashes,
Mending my PC after it crashes,
Girls in bikinis in hot-water springs –
These are a few of my favourite things.

When my horse falls, when my luck swings,
When I'm feeling sad,
I simply remember my favourite things
And then I don't feel so bad.

MY RETIREMENT

I wish I could retire – I'm getting old and weary now,
My bones tell me to give it up, it's time to take a bow.
Yes, I have reached the top rung of my working ladder.
There are many ways I feel it, and one of them's my bladder.

The winters seem to last so long, they add to stress and strain,
And I'm a little less prepared to fight the gales again.
How I long to go fishing in the twilight of my years –
I'm sure no one will miss me or shed those salty tears.

Alas, I cannot go just yet – I haven't earned my pension.
A few more years an' a month or two I must stand the tension.
I can't wait until my time comes to chase hobbies with a passion,
Leave all those ships behind me and ignore the Bristol fashion.

All those craft I sailed in, all the places been –
Round the world a few times, all the places seen –
Let them be just fond memories to recall with idle pleasure
While dozing in my armchair and practising my leisure.

So now I'm growing feeble and a little past my prime,
I'll be a golden oldie and forget the passing time.
I'm tired of hanging round and toiling down the docks,
All hours working down there a-watching of the clocks.

No more sitting at anchor riding out the tide –
I'd much prefer my local bar with a cider by my side,
And in tow with my darling, with no worries in the world,
When I strike my flag from the masthead and stow it neatly furled.

I'll be free to see the grandkids – and hand them back again –
Or perhaps go south on holiday aboard an aeroplane.
I s'pose I should keep healthy and lose a little weight
For the day I cross my Rubicon – it's not too long to wait.

February, 1999

NEW BANKNOTES

So Churchill's on a banknote – that's OK with me,
But I reckon most sincerely there's others we should see.
It's mostly men that's designated, embellished in art form
Upon old Britain's money accepted as the norm.

There are many famous women that earned this special place,
For imprinting on our currency of this island race.
Yes, you say in argument, the Queen is shown a lot,
But she is there by birthright – an automatic spot.

Perhaps our lady admirals are few and far between,
Or females in high industry seldom may be seen.
Just delve into our history to find the brilliant minds –
There you'll see variety and many heroines.

So come on, you responsible for designing notes –
Crack fair the whip for gender that wears the petticoats.
I'm sure the girls don't need me to let their shackles free;
It's just a thought in general to help in c'est la vie.

OUR SOLDIERS

You wear the Kevlar helmet when going on patrol,
Code signs on the flap sheet when Warriors start to roll.
RPGs incoming – expecting, all the time,
Contacts with insurgents or deadly roadside mine.

You Tommies toil in searing heat and dust forever there,
Living out of bergens and flies are everywhere,
Stags of sentry duty neath a sangar's roof of tin,
The cutting edge of combat and training kicking in.

You lads ain't amoral and get on with the job,
Have a kind of system when a mortar does a lob.
Engagement rules are rigid in those stinking lands,
Dicing with the petrol bombs hurled from children's hands.

'All the gear, no idea' is how you see the Yanks,
But occasionally you owe 'em one and nod to give 'em thanks
For coming in with air support in their classic style,
Helping out when danger close in horror-ridden mile.

We know it makes you angry when media get it wrong,
But the public is behind you and has been all along.
Sometimes it ain't that easy to share a point of view,
Unless it's with a mucker that's been through same as you.

Years from now, like other wars – the difference is of age –
Your work is relegated to films or history page,
But for now in infancy, thinking more of home,
The bind falls on your loved ones – when they put down the phone.

Joe Earl, REMF.

SPORT OF KINGS

There is a grace and beauty of a racehorse on the run,
The champions outstanding and galloping for fun,
Giving all and battling till the race is won.
These mighty beasts have heart – names trip off the tongue.

The monster Barracuda, the ease of Never Say Die,
The silver Desert Orchid as he passed his rivals by,
Red Rum – a triple winner upon the National course –
My favourite, Persian Punch, a stubborn gutsy horse.

The spirit of Sea Biscuit, Arkle and Mill Reef,
The wonder of old Generous, who beggared all belief,
The steeplechaser One Man, the famous Golden Miller,
Dawn Run on the chases with Jonjo at the tiller.

Partnered by the jockeys – adding magic to the game –
Gordon Richards, Lester Piggott heading list of fame,
Followed by Dunwoody, Francome and McCoy,
Thornton, Tizzard, Murphy and Fallon since a boy.

Cheeky Frank Dettori, Carson of renown,
Riding out from places like Lambourn county town,
Where Mum was once a stable girl spreading youthful wings
In among the characters that made the sport of kings.

THE BIG BANG

Christine's quite an athlete, and fitter – more than most –
Until the day she didn't see, and walked into a post.
She has a nasty bruise and a cut upon her head –
Couldn't really drive home, so took a walk instead.
Whereupon she called us – gave me quite a shock,
Trying to mop the blood up and keep it off her frock.
So we whisked her down the clinic to see the duty nurse,
In case my captain's training made it bloody worse.
She had a boost of tetanus and a pack of ice,
Then we bought some brandy – that made her feel quite nice.
The moral of this story is not to make Chris frown,
But to keep a special lookout when you go to town,
For all the blooming lamp posts will not stay in place –
They'll jump out to hit you *and smack you in the face.*

MY POETRY

I know it isn't poetry – it isn't even prose.
I'm really very sorry if it travels up your nose.
Shall we call it doggerel?
What do you suppose?

THE EX PATS

Ex-patriots they scamper off – they go to live in Spain
For to escape the fog and cold depressing rain.
The house is sold with furniture and garage sales abound;
The car is filled with personal stuff as they steam from Plymouth Sound.

The Costa Blanca beckons them with a new life to the fore,
With a brand-new villa waiting or apartment with pine door.
But take heed, my friends, and listen before your all is lost
In case with heavy heart, old son, you must count up the cost.

The cloudless skies and burning sun, in relentless way –
Remember you're an Englander – do you want it every day?
It's a lazy life and so laid-back on a poolside plastic chair –
Time to think of family and wish they too were there.

But it's not to be; then you see your life's been split asunder.
Time goes on in relaxing mode, but still one has to wonder
Of a normal day in a northern zone with seasons of the year,
Where the weekend days are different and all your friends are near.

A million Brits are out there on the Blanca or the Sol;
For some the Spanish good life takes a weighty toll.
It's not my imagination, for I came out to see
And speak to many ex-pats, an' it's what they told to me.

For plenty it is perfect – I've no call to shout –
But if you're set on moving, please have a shade of doubt,
For I came, I saw, I pondered by the Mediterranean Sea,
Found so many amigos would fly home with me.

Voya en casa manana.

THE BRIDGE OVER THE RIVER KWAI

I travelled far in Thailand – to heat like a devil's brew,
The steaming hellish cauldron that soldier prisoners knew
When made to build a railway along the River Kwai.
Many men were sent there; many were to die.

Withstanding Jap and jungle, they laid an iron trail,
Each sleeper rates a body left to tell the tale.
Days were long and cruel beneath the Nippon whip,
Malaria and dysentery – no mercy for the sick.

Wearing only rice sacks – no shoes on flinted stone –
Ulcers were abounding, rotting to the bone.
Nights were spent in attap huts with two foot six of space.
Soon to shouts of "Speedo" work resumed apace.

Cutting out the Hellfire Pass, building trestles on the way,
Nearby making quotas – 1,000 yards a day.
By hand they hauled the timber from the woods around,
Digging up the bamboo, levelling out the ground.

They built a bridge to fall down named the Pack of Cards,
Risking death and torture from barbaric guards.
Sabotage was carried out as the structure grew,
While enduring dengue fever, beriberi too.

Hard then to imagine the soldiers' state of mind
As they saw the rail to Burma though the hills unwind.
Relieved to have it finished – an end to mortal toil –
But not to see the enemy shift their troops and oil.

In the soldiers' graveyard that marks those bitter years,
Inscriptions on the stonework witness many tears,
For here the foreign visitor found time will not appease.
Strange though, something's missing – the tourist Japanese.

In June 1942, 61,000 British and Allied troops were put to work by the Imperial Japanese Army to construct a railway line 260 miles (415 kilometres) long in mountainous terrain to link Kanchanburi in Thailand to the railway network in Burma (to supply their army there, thus avoiding the hazardous sea route around Singapore). First estimates by the Japanese suggested it would take at least five years, but under tremendous pressure the POWs were forced to build it in sixteen months at the cost of 16,000 lives.

THE HANDBAG

The handbag is a rare delight – it's like Aladdin's cave.
All sorts of things are hidden there that females like to save.
Basically it's fat, with nice long shoulder strap;
It's weighted down with odds and sods and other stuff like that.

But the lady finds just what she wants deep down amongst her treasure
Of keys and pins and leg-hair wax and metric tapes for measure.
The remnants of forgotten ills with aspirins held so dear,
Birth control and other pills with labels quite unclear.

Calorie counters, cotton buds, old lottery tickets too,
Handkerchiefs and white tissues for visiting the loo,
A book of stamps, a tube of glue, letters from I don't know who,
Horoscopes with personal star, road-tax papers for the car.

Perfume loaded by the box, knitting needles, pairs of socks,
Bank statements, counterfoils, sachet samples, body oils,
Tennis balls and eye mascara, postcards from old Connemara,
Itineraries for keep-fit classes, lipstick and a pair of glasses.

Emery boards, a pot of Vick's, silver tweezers, half a brick,
Screwdriver, spanners, skein of wool, ancient notebook partly full,
Bristle brushes for long tresses, photographs and addresses,
Polo mints and a mobile phone, just in case for texting home.

Chequebook stubs, leather gloves, insect spray for the shrubs,
Driving licence, Waitrose card, cuttings from the paper,
Favourite verse, loaded purse and a windscreen scraper,
Credit cards, safety razor, golden buttons off a blazer.

All these things are lugged around – shuttlecocks as well.
It could be that you need them – you really cannot tell.
So you fellas don't take the mick out of the lady's handbag –
In case of flood, you never know, it's handy as a sandbag.

But best of all it is a friend that's with them every day,
Slung upon the shoulder in a casual way.
And don't forget it is a club – not of the member kind,
But the bag itself when wielded right could change a mugger's mind.

THE LADY GARDENERS

The ladies love their gardens – work hard to get it right,
And even graft by moonlight till late into the night.
They weed and dig and sow and labour all the day,
Wearing bright-red wellies to keep the mud at bay.

There's watering cans and hosepipes and a lethal garden rake,
And a huge great pile of rubbish left by the garden gate.
Donning faded blue jeans and a very ancient coat,
They start a-cultivating while humming a cheerful note.

Attacking bits offending where dreaded weeds abound,
Emptying sacks of this and that, spreading contents on the ground.
They are so very careful tending flowers and the posies,
And fit a glove before they prune bushes and the roses.

They go into the garden shed and heave with all their might,
Emerging with a squirty thing for spraying on the blight.
Then they find some pellets for killing all the slugs,
Plus loads and loads of powdered stuff for fighting off the bugs.

Now, in this little haven the ants they build their nest,
But a well-aimed kick from a size-6 boot sends it flying west.
The cat he gives a wide berth cos he's seen the action,
For if the mistress catches him he'll probably end in traction.

For a few weeks in the summer the lady looks for rain,
But it's the ancient god of Horus that I pray to once again.
I like to watch the gardening; I often give advice,
But some of the replies I get – well, they're not always very nice.

So much time is taken up – no time to cook the dinners.
I'm forced to wander down the pub to join the other sinners.
But later in our greenery where eating apples grow,
We lounge and view the scenery from the patio.

I reckon they are marvellous – I'd like to wish them well
For toiling at the hard tasks and making life so swell.
They say all this horticultural stuff is good for you and me,
So while you're working on the lawn I'll sit beneath the tree!

THE BRIDES

A boy came up to see his dad and said, "I want to marry."
"Fair do's," he says to him. "You're twenty-four, why tarry?"
Then he told him who it was: young Jane from out the valley.
"I'm sorry, son, it can't be done – for her mother when I kissed her

"Bewitched me long and led me on – you see, young Jane's your sister."
Broken-hearted he departed, cursing his old dad,
Till one day he returned to say, "I am a lucky lad.
I've found a girl I'd like to wed – it's Joan from ancient boyhood."

His father, looking pale and drawn, to his feet he slowly stood.
"It's time to wed," he sagely said, "you must be twenty-seven,
But my wicked youth and awful truth I really must explain."
He told him of Joan's mother – his voice in earnest pain.

On he went, but the upshot was – I expect that you may gather –
The sequel was, of course, he was her secret father.
Sure stricken now his shocked son fled and tried his grief to smother.
He couldn't stop and blurted out the story to his mother.

"Oh, Mama dear, my love life's doomed to slaughter,
For if I choose another wife 'tis probably his daughter."
"Cheer up," she said. "You marry who you'd rather,
For I as well the truth will tell: your dad is not your father."

THE SOMME

What ghosts are these as I walk the Somme?
I sense the slaughter by bullet and bomb.
Such melancholy churns, but there is no hating,
For nature's friend is time and waiting.
The barbed wire has gone, the grass is growing,
In no-man's-land the farmer's sowing.

The Big Push – Serre stands right ahead,
My father too felled, among the dead,
Easy targets of enfilade.
No higher price than this was paid.
Bravely walking, their guns at port,
He survived – but cut down short.

Long and painful death was near;
He did recover – that's why I'm here.
I found the spot where Dad's war ended;
Not far away, graves well tended.

These are the ghosts as I walk the Somme,
The pals, his friends, his men, – so long.

October 1999

This verse was written after visiting the part of no-man's-land where my father lay wounded on 1 July 1916: Lieutenant F. C. Earl, 30303, aged twenty-one, 12th Battalion Yorks & Lancs.

THE MENIN GATE, YPRES

There was an awful tragic feature of the First World War,
Captured here in 'Wipers' at its city door.
Only names remain in a chiselled state,
Lasting long in testament upon the Menin Gate.

Once these words were soldiers, husbands, brothers, sons,
All to perish somehow if not by hungry guns.
The telegrams delivered, though the heart was stilled –
A little hope perhaps when 'Missing, Believed Killed'.

The last ray then extinguished when welcome peace reborn,
There was no grave to visit – outlook so forlorn.
No resting place to shed a tear, or token left above –
Just a void of sadness and abject grieving love.

The salient kept its secrets – guards its very own –
Few individual crosses or inscriptions set in stone.
So then was built a monument to mark the episode,
Topped with British lion looking down the Menin Road.

Mention by a poet popular at the time:
He called the arch a sepulchre and put it down to crime,
For the carnage of our forces – the total number stuns;
Still it was not big enough though 20,000 tons.

At unveiling of this monument the generals made it clear,
"These soldiers are not missing – they are resting here."
In memory of our dead, vanquished in that fight,
We stand to heed the last post, sounded every night.

Blomfield's memorial combines the architectural features of a classical victory arch and a mausoleum, and it contains, inside and out, huge panels into which are carved the names of the 54,896 officers and men of the Commonwealth forces who died in the Ypres Salient area and who have no known graves. This figure, however, does not represent all the missing from this area. It was found that the Menin Gate, immense though it is, was not large enough to hold the names of all the missing. The names recorded on the gate's panels are those of men who died in the area between the outbreak of war in 1914 and 15 August 1917. The names of a further 34,984 of the missing – those who died between 16 August 1917 and the end of the war – are recorded on carved panels at Tyne Cot Cemetery, on the slopes just below Passchendaele.

THE LAST POST

I've listened at the Menin Gate,
I've heard it on parade,
It's sounded over many ships
And barracks' palisade.

The bugle or the trumpet
Convey the silver notes
Rolling over graveyards,
And duty it emotes.

Compelling is the symbol
Here and overseas,
Gripping at the heart,
A weakening of the knees.

For sure I think of heroes,
The injured and the lost –
Incredible the number,
Beyond belief the cost.

The playing of the last post
With humble due respect
Is our salute to heritage
In freedom we expect.

THE ULSTER 36TH DIVISION 1916

Early on Lord Kitchener, inspecting on the green,
Stated that the Ulstermen were the finest he had seen.
They were the Irish Rifles and the Royal Fusiliers,
Including Inniskillings and the Tyrone Volunteers.

On July the 1st the Big Push saw the Irish troops,
The 36th Division, opposing German groups.
Many miles along the Somme our boys stood the test,
Ulster's proud division making up the best.

Facing stiff defences from Schwaben's tough redoubt,
The Ulsters fought for high ground mid carnage all about.
Feats were incomparable among the spilling blood,
Achieved by unsung heroes in that foreign mud.

Silencing machine guns, fighting hand-to-hand,
They took the German trenches – there they made a stand.
But then trapped in a salient, when distant flanks were lost,
Suffered fire on three sides at enormous cost.

Companies were wiped out; the Ulsters carried on.
Over dead and dying they reformed and fought along.
Soldiers caught in enfilade, shellfire did for more –
Still this brave division held on at the fore.

Dreadful though the outcome, foundations now were laid –
The enemy was shattered by harm the Ulsters made.
On went the day so lethal, for objectives seized,
That won acclaim for gallantry including four VCs.

A tower stands in County Down, where lads trained for glory;
Near Thiepval Wood a replica, built to tell the story
Of the red-hand badge of courage and fighting all the way,
And the sacrifice of brave men – for peace we have today.

HOW TO WEAR A POPPY!

When we buy a poppy, approaching Remembrance Day,
There's a method we should sport it – in a special way.
Don't show it off too early, as politicians do,
Or have it on your right side – that is quite wrong too.

Place it on your left side, so others will not mock.
Make sure the leaf that's with it is eleven of the clock.
I reckon it's noteworthy to pin it on correct
When donning this fine emblem, expressing your respect.

Of course it's not compulsory, but that's the way I see.
One reason why you're wearing it is because we're free.

WIMBORDOM

I don't understand that Wimbledon game –
One that's played by a couple in pain;
They won't ask a person and say "Game, it's agreed."
They find 'em from somewhere and call 'em a seed.

The balls are swiped at a metre-high net –
Backwards and forwards, causing a crick in the neck.
They grunt and they groan, throw hands in the air,
Run the wrong way and seem to despair.

They don't play with one ball to build up a score –
There's dozens of 'em all over the floor;
Then a few more they stick in their drawers,
While watchers must clap and show their applause.

The tally is kept – not just one, two, three,
But love and deuce and advantage to me.
Then they go swatting with bat thing in hand,
While holding their hair back with a large 'lastic band.

A ball hits the line with a slight puff of dust,
Then one of the players goes mad in disgust.
The chap named the umpire sits on a high stool,
He sticks up a finger when there's a break in the rule.

Then he shouts something like "Game, match and set,"
So they sit down with towels and stare at the net.
Ladies that play go flashing their knickers,
And that brings a blush to broad-minded vicars.

There's strawberries galore at £10 a punnet –
It's blatant extortion by the gangsters that run it.
I wouldn't watch this game for minutes on end –
The antics would send me right round the bend.

So you schoolkids and housewives and royal-box toff,
Don't bother going – I've heard it's rained off.

WOOKY

Wooky is our pussycat, his fur is smoky grey,
And when we're in the kitchen he's always in the way.
He generally has some food down in a saucer on the floor,
But then he's nosing in the fridge, trying to find some more.

Well, we give in and feed him – what a ruddy nerve!
Because he will not eat it – he's saving in reserve.
He likes to catch a bird or mouse, and then pull off its head;
Then he'll go and have a snooze on top of someone's bed.

Wooky's four feet long in sunshine, when stretched out on the path,
Then he's curled up in a ball in a basket by the bath.
He is a fussy eater, and he isn't very fat.
I threaten that I'll have him shot if he chucks up on the mat.

He jumps up on the table and slides across the polish,
Knocking half the pictures off to earn a sharp admonish.
He can be very naughty, and when no one is looking
He climbs upon our worktop to see what's just been cooking.

A gentle shove with a size-10 boot is all he understands,
Then he has four left feet – you can hear him when he lands.
He falls asleep so quickly you'd think he's in a coma,
But you just watch him come alive when he smells a food aroma!

He doesn't like the cream or milk – it really is so sad –
But when he's offered brandy he laps it up like mad.
He rubs himself all over you – right up to your knees –
And then he jumps upon your lap and spreads his ruddy fleas.

September 1998

THE REASON

There is a point of reason, any time of season,
To think about or write a bit of verse.
I may rhyme a bird of feather
With a bank of yellow heather –
Lo, an unseen hand just changes tack.

Other bards may grace waving fields of corn;
I would rather tall ships sailing round the Horn.
They write of mighty oaks or spreading chestnut trees;
My mind is of tea clippers scudding in the breeze.
They picture golden daffodils – I fully understand –
While couplets come to me of seascapes far from land.
They imbue their flowered pages – sketch the babbling brook –
While seamen and the oceans deck my weathered book.
Since Noah rode the flood, I reckon true in part
The sea is in the blood – if a mariner at heart.

THE CORONAVIRUS

Here I am, locked down again with loss of liberty,
Not in some foreign jail or freighter far at sea,
But in our home like millions more with captive company,
And biding by a strict routine that's safe for you and me.

I've washed both hands so many times since cleaning out my desk,
And slaved hard in the garden on lawns and all the rest.
No crosswords filled or papers read – with naps pertaining to horses;
Missing the sport where games were played on greens or circular courses.

I'm worried a bit for my wine's running out – I need my glass of red.
Perchance to find a volunteer who shares my feelings of dread!
Wholesome is my dry-store list, but I must not seem to be rude,
But a bottle of this and a bottle of that is surely seen as food!

3 April 2020